COSTUME CAVALCADE

689 Examples of Historic Costume in Colour

Henny Harald Hansen

EYRE METHUEN·LONDON

First published as Klaededragtsen Kavalkade
by Politikens Forlag, Copenhagen, in 1954
First English edition published by Methuen & Co Ltd, 19 July 1956
Reprinted five times
Second edition 1972 published by Eyre Methuen Ltd,
11 New Fetter Lane, London EC4P 4EE

S.B.N. 413 28800 5
Plates printed in six-colour photo-lithography by
The Ysel Press Ltd, Deventer, Holland
Text printed Offset Litho in Great Britain by
Cox & Wyman Ltd,
London, Fakenham and Reading

CONTENTS

INTRODUCTION

On the jacket of this book are two rows of figures. The upper row shows the people of the Middle Ages, with their swaying, stylized postures. Men and women are dressed almost identically in long, loose garments. The colours are dull greens, browns and blues.

The figures in the lower row represent the period of the French Revolution. The women's hair is powdered, they are tightly corseted, and they wear long skirts and large hats; the men are slim and are clad in closely fitting breeches and buttoned coats. Here the colours are light and clear, with contrasting notes of black and white. There is a great similarity between the figures in the same row, and a great dissimilarity between the two rows.

Why are the lines and colours of people's clothing so similar in any given period, and what makes fashion change so that costumes of different periods are so unlike each other? The answer lies in what is called period style, which finds expression in the whole mode of life of an era, and is particularly apparent in its art and architecture. Since period style influences furniture, painting, sculpture and all the inanimate objects which surround us, it is natural that people should try to adapt their appearance to their environment, and they do so through the clothes they wear.

The builders of the towering cathedrals of the Middle Ages had such feeling for vertical lines that they extended their costume by means of tall head-dresses and sharply pointed shoes.

In the Renaissance houses and furniture were square and solid, and both men and women wore ample garments to harmonize with the rooms in which they lived.

In the nineteenth century, when furniture was heavily upholstered and the architectural framework of rooms was smothered in thickly draped curtains and portières, women's clothes became so voluminous that it was difficult to discern the outline of the human form underneath. There are many other examples illustrating this principle.

This book attempts to show how from the earliest times up to the present the leaders of a society have always tried to conform in appearance with the great period styles of their day. In other words, we are here concerned with the history of fashion. A fashion is always created by the upper classes and not by the man in the street, just as a style is always created by a country which has achieved a certain pre-eminence. In Europe the centres of fashion have moved from country to country, following any new concentration of political and economic power.

Europe cannot, however, be considered in isolation. The civilizations of antiquity developed round the Mediterranean, and as in those days it was usually much easier to travel by sea than by land, there was a mingling of cultures, an exchange of influences. It would therefore be too much of a simplification to begin with the costumes of Greece and Rome. To understand the development of European costume, we must examine the costume of ancient Egypt, and we must also know something of the costume of Crete, Asia Minor and Syria. All these countries reached a high level of civilization earlier than Europe; their style of dress influenced Greece and Rome and hence became the basis of European costume.

Contemporary fashion designers are often given the credit for creating a new mode, although this is not strictly true. For fashion is never initiated by the designers. It is a manifestation of the prevailing period style which, although sometimes difficult to define, influences costume as well as most other products of human skill. The style of a period has a life of its own, and therefore its own life cycle. It is born, develops to maturity, and, when its possibilities are exhausted, declines, to be succeeded by something young, vigorous and new. The particular talent of fashion designers lies in their sensitivity to what is characteristic of the style of their age. They notice variations of taste the moment they appear, keep their fingers on the pulse of the period, and express themselves in their own medium—dress.

A cavalcade of costume must show costumes as they were worn by contemporaries, for alone they are empty husks. The arrangement of clothing implies a certain mental outlook which, in the costumes of the past, can only be conveyed by showing how they were worn and how they were regarded by their wearers. This is a point which has been borne carefully in mind in the planning of this book.

Costumes and Styles contains nearly 700 illustrations in colour spread over 96 pages. There are about eight illustrations to a page, and each page has, as far as possible, been planned as a whole. All the illustrations are based on contemporary designs.

Up to the end of the eighteenth century, when first fashion plates and then fashion journals began to appear, illustrations of costume can be found only in works of art (Egyptian tomb paintings, Greek vases, illuminated manuscripts of the Middle Ages, Renaissance paintings, etc.).

The illustrations of this book have been taken from all these different sources. They are not copies of the originals, but they are freely adapted from them. Thus, while they exemplify the various types of costume in different periods, they are not to be considered as art reproductions.

The list of illustrations on page 7 gives notes on the originals and, where possible, the names of the artists. This will enable the reader who is interested to find further illustrations for himself which may widen his knowledge of the costume of a particular period.

Henny Harald Hansen

SOME BOOKS ON COSTUME

The following selection of books on costume may prove useful to readers who wish to obtain more detailed information either on the subject as a whole or on the different periods:

General

MAX VON BOEHN. *Modes and Manners* (8 volumes). London. 1909–35.

HERBERT NORRIS. *Costume and Fashion* (5 volumes published). London. 1924–38.

F. M. KELLY and R. SCHWABE. *Historic Costume: a chronicle of fashion in Western Europe, 1490–1790.* London. 1929.

MILLIA DAVENPORT. *The Book of Costume* (2 volumes). New York. 1948.

R. T. WILCOX. *The Mode in Costume.* New York 1948.

DOUGLAS GORSLINE. *What People Wore.* New York. 1952.

RANDLE B. TRUETT. *First Ladies in Fashion.* New York. 1954.

Ancient

M. G. HOUSTON and F. S. HORNBLOWER. *Ancient Egyptian, Assyrian and Persian Costumes and Decorations.* London. 1920.

H. C. BROHOLM and MARGRETHE HALD. *Costumes of the Bronze Age in Denmark.* Copenhagen. 1940.

MARY G. HOUSTON. *Ancient Greek, Roman and Byzantine Costume and Decoration.* London. 1931.

LILLIAN M. WILSON. *The Clothing of the Ancient Romans.* Baltimore. 1938.

Medieval

MARY G. HOUSTON. *Medieval Costume in England and France.* London. 1939.

JOAN EVANS. *Dress in Medieval France.* Oxford. 1952.

C. W. and PHILLIS CUNNINGTON. *Handbook of English Medieval Costume.* London. 1952.

Sixteenth to Eighteenth Centuries

M. LELOIR. *Histoire du Costume de l'antiquité à 1914.* Paris. 1933–49. (The published volumes, numbered VIII–XII, cover the period 1610–1795).

JAMES LAVER (ed.). *Costume of the Western World.* London. 1951. (The six published volumes cover the period 1485–1660.)

C. W. and PHILLIS CUNNINGTON. *Handbook of English Costume in the Sixteenth Century.* London. 1954.

C. W. and PHILLIS CUNNINGTON. *Handbook of English Costume in the Seventeenth Century.* London. 1955.

Nineteenth and Twentieth Centuries

C. WILLETT CUNNINGTON. *English Women's Clothing in the Nineteenth Century.* London. 1937.

C. WILLETT CUNNINGTON. *English Women's Clothing in the Present Century.* London. 1952.

SOURCES USED FOR THE ILLUSTRATIONS

The drawings of the figures in this book have been based on the following works by anonymous or known artists. (Dates are given in the captions to each figure.)

328–329: Hendrick Aerts
330: Sofonisba Anguisciola
331: Unknown artist
332: Nicholas Hilliard
333: Paul van Somer
334: Isaac Oliver
335: Rodrigo de Villandrando
336: Unknown French artist
337: Peter Paul Rubens
338–339: Dirck Hals
340: Diego Velasquez
341: Cornelius Jonson van Ceulen I
342: Diego Velasquez
343: Anton van Dyck
344–345: Dirck Santvoort
346: Anton van Dyck
347: Juan Andrés Ricci
348: Abraham Bosse
349: Frans Hals
350: Diego Velasquez
351: Peter Paul Rubens
352–353: Anton van Dyck
354–355: Frans Hals and Pieter Codde
356: Anton van Dyck
357: Philippe de Champagne
358–359: Gerard ter Borch
360: Diego Velasquez
361: Francisco Zurbaran
362–363: Bartholemeus van der Helst
364–366: Gerard ter Borch
367: Gabriel Metzu

368: Gerard ter Borch
369: Pieter de Hooch
370–371: Diego Velasquez
372–373: Pieter de Hooch
374: Gerard ter Borch
375–376: Pieter de Hooch
377–378: Charles Lebrun
379–380: Tapestry after Charles Lebrun
381–389: Fashion prints
390–393: Nicolas de Largillière
394–406: Antoine Watteau
407–408: Nicolas Lancret
409–410: Jean-François de Troy
411: Nicolas Lancret
412: François Boucher
413–416: Jean-Baptiste Siméon Chardin
417: Unknown artist
418: George des Marées
419–421: Johann Zoffani
422–424: François Hubert Drouais
425: François Boucher
426: Hyacinthe Rigaud
427: Thomas Gainsborough
428: François Boucher
429: Honoré Fragonard
430–459: Fashion prints
460–462: Fashion pictures
463–468: Fashion journals
469–470: Adam Buck
471–689: Fashion journals

The illustrations were drawn by the following artists:

Figs. 1–380: Ebbe Sunesen
Figs. 381–598: Mogens Bryder
Figs. 599–689: Kaj Nørregaard

EGYPT

c. 3000 – 500 B.C.

1–3. Short loin-cloth, *c.* 1900 B.C. – 4. Skirt over loin-cloth, *c.* 1460 B.C. – 5. Skirts and tunic (*kalasiris*), *c.* 1460 B.C. – 6. Transparent tunic and short loin-cloth, *c.* 1460 B.C. – 7. Woman playing harp, *c.* 1460 B.C. – 8. Woman playing flute; transparent tunic over hip-belt of beads, *c.* 1460 B.C. – 9. Tuthmosis I. The short stiff loin-cloth was preserved in the royal dress, *c.* 1490 B.C.

10. Female dress: long, narrow skirt supported by shoulder strap. Male dress: short loin-cloth and transparent tunic, *c.* 1460 B.C. – 11. Bird hunter: pleated loin-cloth under transparent tunic, *c.* 1420 B.C. – 12. Amenophis II wearing cap-shaped crown and sandals, and sitting on his nurse's lap, *c.* 1430 B.C. – 13. Woman playing flute, on her head a perfume cone, *c.* 1300 B.C. – 14. Female slaves dancing, naked except for jewellery, *c.* 1400 B.C. – 15. Woman playing harp, *c.* 1420 B.C. – 16. Wailing women wearing grey, colour of mourning, *c.* 1400 B.C.

17. Daughter of King Akhenaten with characteristically shaped head of her family, *c.* 1360 B.C. –
18. Long narrow skirt and shoulder cape, *c.* 1300 B.C. – 19. High Priest wearing ceremonial leopard
skin and pleated skirt tied outside tunic, *c.* 1300 B.C. – 20. Pleated female dress, skirt and cape
knotted on breast, *c.* 1250 B.C. – 21. Queen Nefertiti wearing pleated dress, *c.* 1250 B.C. – 22. Long
narrow skirt covered with beads, with shoulder straps, *c.* 1250 B.C. – 23. King Rameses III, *c.* 1180
B.C. – 24. Woman's skirt with shoulder straps and sash, *c.* 1180 B.C.

EGYPT
NEIGHBOURING PEOPLES,
c. 1900–1400 B.C.

25. Semite wearing patterned woollen loin-cloth and sandals with straps, *c.* 1900 B.C. – 26. Semitic women wearing patterned woollen dresses, *c.* 1900 B.C. – 27. Syrian ambassador wearing patterned loin-cloth (Cretan style), *c.* 1460 B.C. – 28. Syrian in long-sleeved Asiatic tunic, *c.* 1460 B.C. – 29–30. Syrian ambassadors in robes wound spiral-wise, *c.* 1400 B.C.

THE AEGEAN
c. 2000–1100 B.C.

31. Libation. Long dresses of Syrian origin. Crete, *c.* 1700 B.C. – 32. Man with tight, padded belt and loin-cloth; on his head a goatskin cap. Crete, *c.* 1600 B.C. – 33. Man in short tunic. Greece, *c.* 1400 B.C. – 34. Woman in flounced skirt and short-sleeved jacket. Greece, *c.* 1400 B.C. – 35. Priest-King in 'half skirt', stylized lilies on crown. Crete, *c.* 1600 B.C. – 36. Vase carrier in loin-cloth with network of beads. Crete, *c.* 1700 B.C. – 37. Serpent goddess in long, flounced skirt with short 'half skirt' on top. Short-sleeved jacket leaves breasts bare. Crete, *c.* 1700 B.C.

GREECE
c. 700–150 B.C.

38. Men in cloaks and long *chitons* (linen drapery of tunic form), *c.* 550 B.C. – 39. Short cloak as only garment, *c.* 570 B.C. – 40. Leopard skin worn over short *chiton*, *c.* 570 B.C. – 41. Man wearing long ceremonial *chiton* and cloak, *c.* 570 B.C. – 42. Women wearing close-fitting *peplos* (woollen drapery of tunic form); top edge folded outwards, high belted waist, *c.* 570 B.C.

43. Dionysus, god of wine, in long, pleated *chiton* and large cloak wrapped round body, *c.* 550 B.C.
– 44. Polyxena, the King's daughter, wearing *peplos* fastened with pins at shoulders, *c.* 570 B.C. –
45. Large, draped cloak (*himation*), *c.* 540 B.C. – 46. Man in long, pleated linen *chiton*, *c.* 540 B.C.

47   48   49

50   51   52   53

47. The goddess Athene, *c.* 500 B.C. – 48. The mythical hero Heracles wearing large, draped cloak (*himation*), *c.* 500 B.C. – 49. Pleated linen *chiton* with overfold pulled up over belt, giving blouse effect, *c.* 480 B.C. – 50. Pleated linen *chiton*, the upper edges fastened together to form sleeves, and patterned cloak, *c.* 480 B.C. – 51. Small cloak and hat, *c.* 480 B.C. – 52. Man with large cloak draped over head, *c.* 480 B.C. – 53. Large patterned cloak, *c.* 480 B.C.

54 55 56 57

58 59

54. Warrior in *chiton*, helmet and greaves, *c.* 480 B.C. – 55. Amazon wearing Asiatic costume, including trousers and high cap with ear flaps, *c.* 480 B.C. – 56. Hector, the Trojan hero, puts on his corselet, *c.* 480 B.C. – 57. Queen Hecuba, Hector's mother, wearing *chiton* and cloak, hands him helmet and spear, *c.* 480 B.C. – 58. A sister of Medusa in *chiton* and cloak worn obliquely, *c.* 490 B.C. – 59. The hero Perseus wearing *chiton*, leopard skin, hat with turned-up brim, and boots, *c.* 490 B.C.

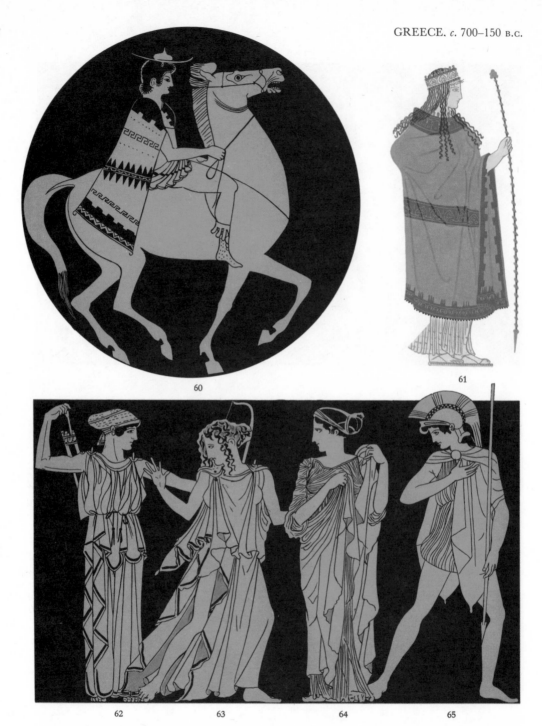

60. Horseman in stiff patterned cloak and flat hat, *c.* 500 B.C. – 61. The goddess Hera wearing pleated linen *chiton*, patterned cloak, sandals and diadem, *c.* 470 B.C. – 62. Full *peplos* falling in many folds, worn open with belt tied over long overfold, *c.* 460 B.C. – 63. *Peplos* open and without belt, as worn by the Spartan women ('the hip-showing ones'), *c.* 430 B.C. – 64. Pleated linen *chiton* and cloak, *c.* 430 B.C. – 65. Warrior in pleated linen *chiton* and small cloak (*chlamys*) fastened with brooch, *c.* 460 B.C.

66. Shepherd carrying child, the *chiton* girded up, *c.* 450 B.C. – 67. Woman wearing *chiton* with vertical stripe and cloak, *c.* 350 B.C. – 68. Man in short *chiton*, *c.* 450 B.C. – 69. Dionysus, god of wine, wearing long pleated *chiton*, upper edges of which are fastened together to form sleeves, and large cloak, *c.* 440 B.C. – 70. Woman wearing full *peplos* falling in many folds; open on right side and with deep overfold, *c.* 440 B.C. – 71. The hero Castor wearing cloak (*chlamys*) fastened with brooch, *c.* 430 B.C. – 72–73. Dancing women in *chitons* fastened like the *peplos*, *c.* 430 B.C.

ITALY
THE ETRUSCANS, *c.* 1000–300 B.C.

74. Woman wearing *chiton* with cloak over head, and pointed shoes, *c.* 550 B.C. – 75. Female dress, *c.* 550 B.C. – 76. Men in long pleated *chitons* and cloaks, *c.* 540 B.C. – 77. Man in long *chiton*, cloak and pointed shoes, *c.* 530 B.C. – 78. Gladiator in short *chiton*, pointed cap and mask, *c.* 530 B.C. 79. Dancing woman in long transparent *chiton*, large blue cloak with red lining, high head-dress and pointed shoes, *c.* 520 B.C.

80. Man and boy flute player, both wearing cloaks, *c.* 500 B.C. – 81. Reclining man wrapped in large cloak, hair bound with fillet, *c.* 520 B.C. – 82. Man with loose shawl round shoulders, *c.* 500 B.C. – 83. Flute player wearing large cloak and sandals, *c.* 500 B.C. – 84. Lyre player in cloak, *c.* 500 B.C. – 85. Dancing woman in long, transparent *chiton* and large cloak, *c.* 500 B.C. – 86. Flute player wearing small shawl and boots, *c.* 500 B.C. – 87. Man in cloak with design of figures, laurel wreath on head, *c.* 300 B.C.

88

ROME
c. 700 B.C.–A.D. 467

89   90   91

88. Women at funeral dancing in a row, *c.* 450 B.C. – 89. Woman wearing sleeveless dress (*tunica*) and cloak (*palla*), *c.* 50 B.C. – 90. Married woman in overdress (*stola*) and veil, *c.* 50 B.C. – 91. Kneeling woman in cloak, seated woman in *tunica*, *c.* 50 B.C.

92. Oldest kind of toga, worn by the 'Arringatore', an Etruscan statue, *c.* 300 B.C. – 93. Toga of Imperial Rome shortly before birth of Christ. – 94. Top layer of toga draped over head from behind, *c.* 10 B.C. – 95. Official wearing two tunics and toga, which is kept in place by its folds forming a wide band over chest, *c.* A.D. 320. – 96. Philosopher in loosely draped large cloak (*pallium*) corresponding to Greek *himation* (see Fig. 45), *c.* 50 B.C. – 97. Woman in *tunica* and cloak, *c.* A.D. 40. – 98. Female dress, *c.* 50 B.C. – 99. Woman playing cithara, *c.* 50 B.C.

BYZANTIUM

c. 300–1450

100. Christ as the Good Shepherd, wearing wide-sleeved tunic (*dalmatica*) with vertical stripes (*clavi*), and cloak, *c.* 450. – 101. *Dalmatica* and cloak, *c.* 450. – 102. Woman wearing tunic and cloak, *c.* 425. – 103. Apostle wearing *dalmatica* and cloak, *c.* 450. – 104. Saint wearing *dalmatica* and cloak, *c.* 450. – 105. Christ depicted in *dalmatica* and cloak, *c.* 520.

106. Soldiers of the Emperor Justinian's bodyguard, *c.* 550. – 107. Civilian dignitaries in tunics and large cloaks fastened with brooches and having a rectangular ornament (*tablion*), *c.* 550. – 108. Emperor Justinian. Knee-length tunic, large cloak with brooch, rectangular ornament, *c.* 550. – 109. Archbishop Maximilian and deacon. The Archbishop wears chasuble and narrow woven band of wool (*pallium*), *c.* 550. – 110. Courtiers in tunics and large cloaks with brooches and *tablion, c.* 550. – 111. Empress Theodora. Tunic, large cloak with brooch, jewelled collar and diadem, *c.* 550. – 112–13. Court ladies wearing long tunics of materials woven with gold thread and shawls, *c.* 550.

114. St. Agnes. Two tunics and veil, *c.* 550. – 115. St. Peter in *dalmatica* with *clavi* and cloak, *c.* 530. – 116–17. Saints in tunics and cloaks, *c.* 530. – 118. Female saint in tunic and cloak, *c.* 750. – 119. Empress Theophano. Tunic and cloak adorned with jewels, *c.* 800. – 120. *Dalmatica* with vertical stripes (*clavi*) ending below in circular ornaments (*orbiculi*), *c.* 850. – 121. Emperor. Long *tunica* adorned with jewels; jewelled band wound round body, *c.* 960.

122. *Tunica,* cloak and red boots studded with jewels, *c.* 1000. – 123–24. Emperor and Empress in identical costumes, stiff with gold embroidery and applied jewels, *c.* 1080. – 125. Daniel in the lion's den, wearing stylized version of Roman soldier's uniform, *c.* 1100. – 126. Horşeman dressed as Roman soldier, *c.* 1100. – 127. Lot and his daughter escaping from Sodom, in the Byzantine style, *c.* 1180.

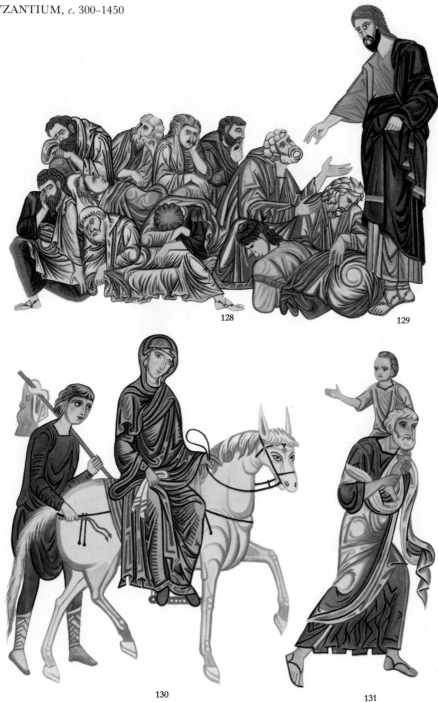

128. Biblical figures in the Byzantine style: the sleeping disciples wrapped in large cloaks, *c.* 1200. –
129. Christ on the Mount of Olives; *dalmatica* and cloak, *c.* 1200. – 130. The Flight into Egypt: the
Virgin in tunic and cloak drawn over her head, *c.* 1130. – 131. Joseph with the child Jesus: Joseph
in *dalmatica* and cloak, traditional dress of sacred figures; child in *dalmatica* only, *c.* 1130

132–33. Archangels Michael and Gabriel, depicted in embroidered costumes, *c.* 1375. – 134–35. Russian saints, Princes Boris and Gleb, killed in 1015. Instead of a cloak, Boris wears an Asiatic sleeved caftan over his shoulders, *c.* 1400. – 136–37. Long tunics, fur-lined semi-circular cloaks, and high boots of red leather, *c.* 1400. – 138–39. Russian saints in ecclesiastical robes, *c.* 1500.

THE MIDDLE AGES
ROMANESQUE PERIOD, *c.* 800–1200

140. Medieval interpretation of Madonna and Child. Long tunic and veil. Ireland, *c.* 890. – 141. Saint. Long-sleeved tunic and cloak. Ireland, *c.* 890. – 142. Saint in tunic and cloak. Ireland, *c.* 890. – 143. Emperor Otto III in coronation robes. Two long tunics and large cloak fastened with brooch on right shoulder, *c.* 1000. – 144. Shepherd in leggings, short tunic and cloak, *c.* 1000. – 145. Bodyguard in leggings, short tunic and cloak fastened with brooch, *c.* 1000.

146. Apostle in tunic and cloak, *c.* 1100. – 147. Horseman in short tunic and leggings, *c.* 1100. –
148. Man in long leggings and short tunic, *c.* 1100. – 149. Woman wearing long tunic, cloak with
brooch and kerchief, *c.* 1100. – 150. Warrior in leggings, short tunic and cloak fastened with brooch,
c. 1100.

151 152 153 154

155 156 157 158

151. Male costumes: leggings, short tunic, small cloak fastened with brooch, *c.* 1150. – 152. Warrior in knee-length mail-shirt with skirt slit so that it resembles a pair of short trousers, *c.* 1150. – 153. Royal costume. Long tunic and large cloak fastened with brooch under chin, *c.* 1150. – 154. Male costume, *c.* 1150. – 155. Saint in tunic and cloak, *c.* 1110. – 156. Clerical dress, *c.* 1110. – 157. Bishop, *c.* 1110. – 158. Madonna and Child, costume of about 1250.

159. Pilgrim in long tunic, closed cloak with hood, and hat, *c.* 1200. – 160. Man in tunic and cloak, *c.* 1250. – 161. Both figures wear long tunics of *c.* 1250. – 162–63. Closed cloaks with hoods, *c.* 1250. – 164. Short tunic and leggings with spiral leg-bandages, *c.* 1200. – 165. Female costumes: tunics, cloaks and veils, *c.* 1175. – 166. Men, one wearing cloak and hood with elongated point, *c.* 1200.

167–68. Alexander the Great in single combat, depicted as medieval crusader, *c.* 1200. – 169–70. Men wearing leggings, short tunics and small cloaks, *c.* 1200. – 171. One of the Three Kings, wearing long tunic and cloak, *c.* 1200. – 172. The Virgin in long, loose tunic and cloak, *c.* 1200. – 173. One of the Three Kings in costume of *c.* 1200.

174. Married woman wearing coif, gown with train and cloak, *c.* 1250. – 175–76. Knights in chain-mail, *c.* 1250. – 177. King. Tunic, sleeveless surcoat, *c.* 1250. – 178. Jew wearing pointed hat, obligatory for his race in the Middle Ages, *c.* 1250. – 179. Man wearing undertunic with narrow sleeves, sleeveless surcoat and cloak, his hair in loose curls, *c.* 1250. – 180–81. Youth with girl wearing long gown with train and virgin's crown, *c.* 1250.

182–83. Troubadour handing poem to his lady. Both wear fur-lined cloaks, *c.* 1325. – 184–85. Tryst. Both have garlands on their heads and wear undertunics and sleeveless surcoats, *c.* 1325. – 186 – 87. Knight receiving helmet from his lady's hand, his device embroidered on his sleeveless surcoat, *c.* 1325. – 188. Merchant, *c.* 1325. – 189. Jew wearing fur-lined cloak and pointed hat, *c.* 1325.

190. Long tunic girt up, showing hose; hooded cloak reduced to pointed hood with shoulder-cape, *c.* 1325. – 191. Same dress, hat with turned-up brim, *c.* 1325. – 192. Knight with hawk, *c.* 1325. – 193. Particoloured dress (*mi-parti*), *c.* 1325. – 194. Tall hat with turned-up brim, and cape, *c.* 1325. – 195. Man with tunic girded up and bonnet-shaped head-dress, *c.* 1325. – 196. Married woman with kerchief, undergown with long narrow sleeves and sleeveless surcoat, *c.* 1325.

197   198

199   200   201

197. Noble wearing chain-mail and sleeveless surcoat. Coat-of-arms on surcoat and shield, *c.* 1290.
– 198. Saint in chain-mail and sleeveless surcoat; cross on shield and surcoat, *c.* 1290. – 199. Knight.
Coat-of-arms on surcoat, helmet, saddle and horse-trapper, *c.* 1340. – 200. Female dress. Undergown
and sleeveless, particoloured surcoat showing introduction of deep armholes, 'The windows of hell'
(*fenêtres d'enfer*), *c.* 1340. – 201. Female dress. Undergown with narrow sleeves, surcoat with device
woven into fabric, *c.* 1340.

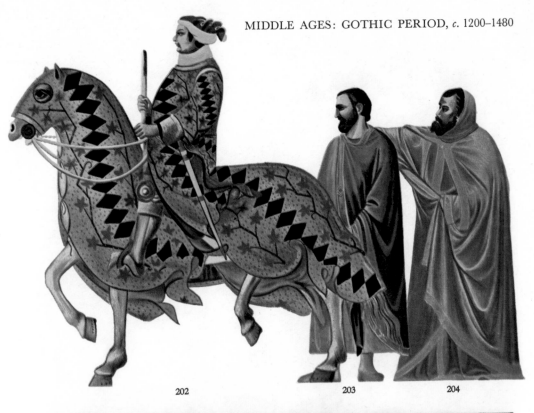

202. Italian military commander (*condottiere*). Over his plate-armour a surcoat of same material as horse-trapper, 1328. – 203–4. Apostles portrayed in their traditional garb, *dalmatica* and cloak, *c.* 1320. – 205. Girl with garland of flowers in hair, wearing fur-edged surcoat, *c.* 1440. – 206. Youth wearing short undertunic and sleeveless surcoat dagged into oak-leaf patterns at hem, *c.* 1440. – 207. Female dress with large hanging sleeves dagged into oak-leaf patterns along edge, *c.* 1440. – 208. Youth wearing dagged undertunic with hip-belt, *c.* 1440.

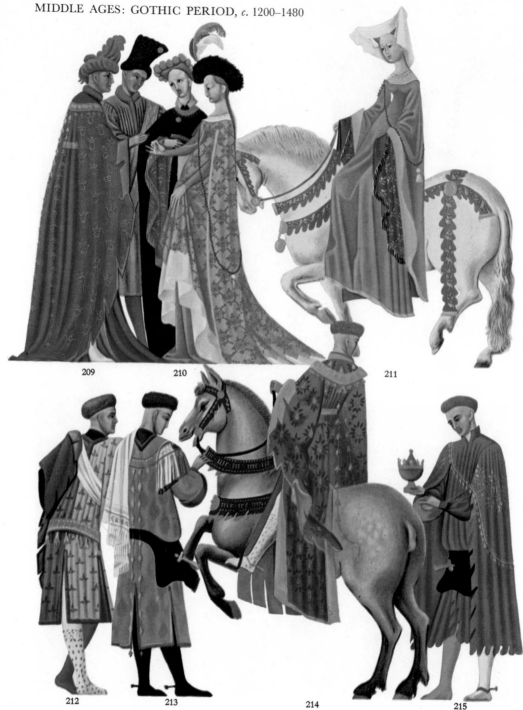

209. Men wearing voluminous gowns (*houppelande*) with trailing sleeves dagged along edge, *c.* 1410. – 210. Female costume: two gowns with trains and long hanging sleeves, *c.* 1410. – 211. Two gowns with long funnel-shaped sleeves, the head-dress wider than it is high, *c.* 1410. – 212. Male costume, particoloured, with hip-belt, *c.* 1410. – 213. Brocaded coat with slits, and hip-belt, *c.* 1410. – 214. Knight wearing *houppelande*, *c.* 1410. – 215. Male dress with dagged edges and hip-belt, *c.* 1410.

216. Horseman wearing fur cap and long, slit fur-lined coat, *c.* 1430. – 217. Man wearing mantle and turban-like hood with liripipe hanging over shoulder, *c.* 1430. – 218. Woman wearing kerchief with fluted edges and fur-trimmed *houppelande*, held up, with dagged, hanging sleeves, 1434. – 219. Male dress with hanging sleeves and large flat hat with liripipe hanging down, *c.* 1460. – 220. Man with hanging sleeves, fitted hose, black shoes, *c.* 1460. – 221. Archer wearing short doublet and hose sewn together to make tight-fitting 'trousers', with codpiece, 1475. – 222. Archer in tunic and cloak. Hose have been untied from belt and pulled down, *c.* 1475.

223. Man wearing tight-fitting hose, short doublet with skirt, padded shoulders (*mahoitres*) and pointed shoes, *c.* 1460. – 224. Herald wearing high Burgundian cap, *c.* 1460. – 225. Female dresses: the first, a low-cut dress with ermine trimming, long sleeves covering hands, voluminous train, high waist-line with broad belt; conical head-dress (*hennin*) with starched linen arranged high on head, *c.* 1460. – 226. Ladies' dresses with trains: the first a steeple *hennin* with flowing veil, *c.* 1460. – 227. Knight arrayed for tournament, *c.* 1460.

228   229   230   231

232

228. Men wearing hose sewn together to make tight-fitting 'trousers', with codpiece and pointed shoes. One man wears high Burgundian cap, *c.* 1460. – 229. Kneeling man with cape of miniver, *c.* 1460. – 230. Female dress: steeple *hennin* with starched linen wings. Man wearing long coat, *c.* 1460. – 231. Man wearing long gown and flat hat with liripipe over shoulder, *c.* 1460. – 232. Knight riding in tournament, *c.* 1460.

THE RENAISSANCE
ITALIAN FASHIONS, *c.* 1480–1510

233. Knight in armour, turban head-dress, and cloak of brocade, *c.* 1460. – 234. Traveller, *c.* 1425. – 235. Woman wearing long dress and cloak over head, *c.* 1425. – 236. Man in short doublet, bare-legged, *c.* 1425. – 237. St. George depicted as warrior in armour, with pleated cloak and large, flat straw hat, *c.* 1460.

238. Young man wearing knee-length outer tunic (*cotehardie*) of patterned velvet, and turban hat, *c.* 1425. – 239. Young man wearing knee-length tunic (*cotehardie*), with full sleeves and turban, *c.* 1425. – 240. Horseman in armour, boy in pleated jerkin, *c.* 1450. – 241. Man wearing caught-up outer tunic with hose pulled down and strap under instep, 1469. – 242. Knight in armour with closed helmet, *c.* 1450. – 243. Man in cloak and large flat hat with band hanging behind (liripipe), *c.* 1450. – 244. Woman in blue dress and pink cloak, *c.* 1450.

245 246 247

248 249 250 251 252

245–46. Men wearing pleated doublets with sleeves padded at shoulders, round hats and tight-fitting hose, *c.* 1455. – 247. Peasant with unbuttoned doublet over shirt, hose pulled down, ankle-length boots, *c.* 1450. – 248. Man wearing jerkin with loosely hanging ornamental sleeves, *c.* 1450. – 249. Woman wearing gown with train and hanging sleeves, *c.* 1450. – 250. Woman wearing dress and trailing cloak dagged along edge, *c.* 1450. – 251. Man wearing large cloak and high hat, wider at top, *c.* 1450. – 252. Male costume, *c.* 1450.

253. Man wearing pleated doublet with sleeves wide at shoulders, 1457. – 254. Man wearing doublet with small collar, *c.* 1470. – 255. Woman wearing kerchief, *c.* 1475. – 256. Woman with dress girt up, *c.* 1490. – 257. Woman wearing kerchief, *c.* 1490. – 258. Woman wearing kerchief and long sleeves tied to dress at shoulders, *c.* 1490. – 259. Woman wearing richly folding dress without train, laced in front and along underarm of sleeves, which are tied to dress, *c.* 1490. – 260. Woman with kerchief, *c.* 1490.

261. Man wearing short doublet, flat cap and particoloured hose, *c.* 1490. – 262. Man wearing short gown of brocade with long, hanging sleeves and large hat with turned-up brim, *c.* 1490. – 263. Man wearing short gown and flat cap, *c.* 1490. – 264. Man wearing short coat and small cap, hair shoulder-length, finely pleated shirt visible in front, *c.* 1490. – 265. Man wearing short skirtless jacket, and hose sewn together to form tight-fitting trousers, *c.* 1490. – 266. Man wearing long gown and cap, *c.* 1490. – 267. Woman wearing dress with sleeves tied on, *c.* 1490. – 268. Men in clothes cut very full, falling in many folds, hair shoulder-length, *c.* 1490.

269. Reclining woman in white dress with gold trimming, *c.* 1490. – 270. Man in low-cut doublet with sleeves tied on, striped hose and blue boots, *c.* 1500. – 271. Monastic habit, 1505. – 272. Man wrapped in large cloak wearing cap, hair shoulder length, 1505. – 273. Man wearing coat with shoulder-cape, and hat with turned-up brim, 1505. – 274. Woman wearing sleeveless coat and dress with square neckline filled in by *chemisette*; slashed sleeves, 1505. – 275. Man wearing cap, cloak, doublet and hose with codpiece, 1505. – 276. Woman wearing large cloak, her hair in a net, 1505.

277. Woman wearing hood-shaped head-dress and two gowns, the top one split; square neckline, *c.* 1495. – 278. Man in particoloured doublet with pleated skirt, particoloured hose, broad-toed shoes and wide-brimmed cap, *c.* 1495. – 279. Man wearing long boots and wide-brimmed cap, *c.* 1500. – 280. Man wearing long boots and small cap, *c.* 1500. – 281. Man wearing full cloak, broad-toed shoes and wide-brimmed cap over skull-cap, *c.* 1510. – 282. Youth with long hair wearing low-cut tunic, *c.* 1500. – 283. Man in armour, surcoat with hanging sleeves, wide-brimmed cap with ostrich feather, *c.* 1500. – 284. Man in hose, short coat and wide-brimmed cap with ostrich feathers, *c.* 1500.

285. Woman shown in old-fashioned Gothic dress with wide armholes in outer gown, but with low head-dress, *c.* 1500. – 286. Man wearing large cloak, *c.* 1510. – 287. Woman wearing dress with slashed sleeves and bodice, *c.* 1500. – 288. Man wearing long outer gown of patterned velvet and wide-brimmed cap, *c.* 1510.   289. Man dancing, wide-brimmed cap over skull-cap, slashed sleeves and hose, *c.* 1510. – 290. Man with short hair, and beard, *c.* 1510. – 291. Man wearing large, ermine-lined cloak and knee-length tunic of patterned velvet, *c.* 1500. – 292. Woman shown in old-fashioned Gothic dress, but with flat head-dress, *c.* 1510.

293.   294.   295.   296.

297.   298.   299.

293. Hunter in doublet, hose and hat with ostrich feather, c. 1510. – 294. Woman shown in old-fashioned Gothic dress with hood worn as bonnet, c. 1510. – 295. Woman wearing pleated cloak and kerchief, 1500. – 296. Woman wearing bonnet, pleated apron and shoulder-cape, 1500. – 297. Woman shown in old-fashioned Gothic dress, but with flat head-dress, c. 1510. – 298. Man wearing doublet, slashed hose and cap, c. 1510. – 299. Executioner with short hair, and beard, wearing doublet, shirt and hose sewn together to form trousers, c. 1510.

300. Woman wearing ceremonial dress with train and kerchief, 1500. – 301. Female dress with sleeves in sections, laced together, 1506. – 302. Man wearing short jacket with slashed sleeves and shoes, hat brim turned up, 1503. – 303. Beggar in ragged clothing, *c.* 1510. – 304. Nobleman in slashed costume and broad-toed shoes, 1514. – 305. Woman wearing cap with ostrich feathers, 1514. – 306. Female dress with square neckline and laced-in waist, *c.* 1514. – 307. Woman wearing horizontally striped dress, puffed sleeves and bonnet head-dress, *c.* 1523.

308 309 310

311 312 313

308. Man wearing cap, short fur-lined gown, long-skirted doublet and broad-toed shoes, 1533. –
309. Woman wearing black, high-necked dress and caftan-like coat, 1538. – 310. Bishop, 1533. –
311. Henry VIII in long skirted doublet leaving codpiece exposed, short gown with hanging sleeves,
broad-toed shoes, and cap, 1537. – 312. Woman wearing bonnet head-dress, gown and undergown,
1539. – 313. Man wearing cap, short gown, doublet, short puffed breeches with codpiece, and shirt
with high collar, *c.* 1540.

314. Princess, later Queen, Elizabeth of England, in costume consisting of gown and undergown over conical farthingale, *c.* 1547. – 315. Male dress, 1548. – 316. Youth wearing high-necked doublet with small ruff and circular fur-lined cloak, *c.* 1555. – 317. Catherine de Medici wearing dress embroidered with jewels, *c.* 1555. – 318. Boy's costume, *c.* 1550. – 319. Man wearing high-necked doublet with skirt and shoulder-wings, stuffed trunk hose and high hat, 1552. – 320. Girl's dress, 1554. – 321. Man's dress, 1564.

322   323   324   325

326   327   328   329

322. Peasant musician, 1565. – 323. Woman wearing ruff and open gown with shoulder-wings over farthingale, *c.* 1575. – 324. Man in gorget and 'peascod' jerkin, 1577. – 325. Spanish princess with ruff, and gown (*saya*) over conical farthingale, *c.* 1585. – 326. Woman wearing padded roll round hips under gown, *c.* 1580. – 327. Man wearing padded doublet to form 'peascod belly', and ruff, *c.* 1580. – 328. Female dress with ruff, 1602. – 329. Male costume, 1602.

330   331   332

333   334   335

330. Man wearing armour, c. 1600. – 331. Queen Elizabeth I wearing drum-shaped farthingale under long-waisted gown adorned with jewels, and with wired lace collar, 1592. – 332. Elizabethan courtier wearing fancy dress with 'peascod belly', c. 1590. – 333. Woman's dress with saffron-coloured collar and cuffs, 1617. – 334. Man wearing stiff semi-circular lace collar and cuffs, 1616. – 335. Man wearing cloak, doublet with skirt, padded short breeches, 'millstone ruff' and cuffs to match, c. 1615.

BAROQUE
c. 1620–1715

336. Anne of Austria in court dress with 'millstone ruff' of several layers of starched lace, *c.* 1625. – 337. Boy's costume with plain, falling lace collar, rosettes on shoes, and garters, 1625. – 338. Soft falling ruff, large felt hat, doublet with divided skirt, full loose breeches, and garters with rosettes, *c.* 1630. – 339. Woman wearing 'millstone ruff', the farthingale replaced by several skirts, *c.* 1630. – 340. Man in black costume with small, round, stiff collar (*golilla*), 1633. – 341. Girl's dress, 1631. – 342. Man in embroidered costume with small, round, stiff collar (*golilla*), 1633. – 343. Female dress with plain lace collar and cuffs, *c.* 1630.

344 345 346 347

348 349 350 351

344. Man wearing lace collar and cuffs, short-waisted doublet, narrow trousers, boots with boot hose and lace tops, *c.* 1635. – 345. Woman wearing high-waisted dress with lace collar and cuffs; rosettes on sleeves and belt, *c.* 1635. – 346. Man wearing lace collar over cuirass, 1635. – 347. Man wearing lace collar, long hair and boots, 1635. – 348. Man wearing lace collar and boot hose with lace tops; long hair plaited in pigtails (*cadenettes*), 1635. – 349. Man wearing unstarched ruff, 1640. — 350. Boy's hunting costume, 1635. – 351. Woman's costume with broad-brimmed felt hat and ostrich feather, the overdress looped up, 1635.

352. Woman wearing lace collar and cuffs, a long lock of hair on left shoulder, 1635. – 353. Man with lace collar and high-heeled leather boots, *c.* 1635. – 354–55. Men wearing lace collars, lace tops on boot hose, and large taffeta sashes round waist, 1637. – 356. William II of Orange and his child bride, both with lace collars, the girl with pearls, 1641. – 357. Cardinal Richelieu, 1640.

358. Man in black costume, broad-brimmed felt hat with pointed crown, and plain white collar, 1642. – 359. Woman wearing black costume with plain white collar round shoulders, and plain white cuffs, 1642. — 360. Court jester in old-fashioned dress based on 'the Spanish fashion', 1644. – 361. Woman's dress, *c.* 1645. – 362. Man wearing short-waisted doublet with slashed sleeves and sash, long narrow breeches fastened with visible buttons, leather boots, collar and cuffs edged with plain lace, 1650. – 363. Elderly man wearing soft ruff, 1650. – 364. Woman's dress, 1665. – 365. Man wearing breeches decorated with ribbons, 1665.

366   367   368   369

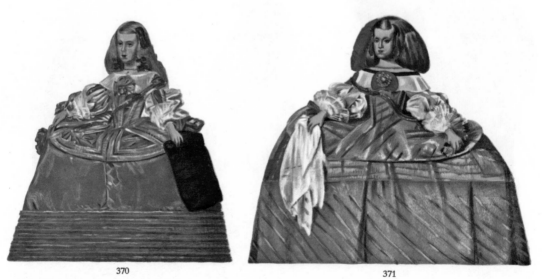

370   371

366–68. Women's dresses with low, round neckline, large three-quarter sleeves, and natural waist line, 1660. – 369. Man wearing skirt-like Rhinegrave breeches and ruffles below knees, 1658. – 370. Spanish princess in drum-shaped farthingale worn in Spain all through seventeenth century with oval neckline and large sleeves. In her hand a muff, 1659. – 371. Spanish princess wearing farthingale of oval shape (flat front and back), 1660.

372. Dress of citizen's wife, 1658. – 373. Girl's dress, 1658. – 374. Man with long hair, felt hat with pointed crown, rectangular white collar with lace design, round cloak, jacket reduced to bolero, shirt, much of it visible, skirt-shaped Rhinegrave breeches, ruffles below knee, shoes with bows, 1665. – 375. Female dress, 1665. – 376. Man wearing Rhinegrave breeches trimmed with ribbon bows (*galants*), 1665. – 377–78. Men wearing Rhinegrave breeches and short jackets, 1680. – 379–80. Men wearing knee-breeches (*culotte*) trimmed with ribbon bows, and short coats (*casaque*), *c.* 1685.

381. Man wearing periwig, coat (*justaucorps*) with large cuffs and pocket-flaps, lace cravat, and high-heeled shoes, *c.* 1690. – 382. Woman's dress, *c.* 1690. – 383. Man in night-cap, a wig placed on stand, *c.* 1690. – 384. Man wearing long coat (*justaucorps*), long waistcoat and stockings pulled over breeches (*culotte*), lace cravat, periwig and three-cornered hat, *c.* 1695. – 385. Woman wearing high head-dress (*fontange*), ornamental apron and patches, *c.* 1695. – 386. Woman wearing looped-up gown with train (*manteau*), skirt (*jupe*) with flounces (*falbalas*), long gloves and head-dress (*fontange*), *c.* 1695.

387. Woman wearing looped-up gown (*manteau*), high head-dress (*fontange*), sleeves of chemise ending in frills (*engageantes*) at elbows, *c.* 1695. – 388. Woman wearing loose-fitting house-coat, later called *contouche*, and high head-dress (*fontange*), *c.* 1705. – 389. Man's costume, *c.* 1705. – 390. Lady with black *fontange*, and child in leading strings, 1712. – 391. Powdered periwig, 1712. – 392. Louis XIV wearing periwig with peaks rising either side of parting and clad in brown, the Sun King's favourite colour, 1712. – 393. Coat (*justaucorps*), with cuffs of gold brocade and waistcoat to match; under arm, a three-cornered hat, 1712.

FRENCH REGENCY
c. 1715–1730

394   395   396

397   398   399

394. Female dress, *c.* 1715. – 395. Woman with plain coiffure and loose-fitting gown (*contouche*), *c.* 1715. – 396. Man's dress, *c.* 1715. – 397. Woman with plain coiffure and small cap, dressed in long, loose-hanging gown (*contouche*) over conical hoop petticoat (*panier*), 1718. – 598. Woman with plain coiffure, small cap and striped dress over hoop petticoat (*panier*); round her neck a loosely tied lace scarf, 1718. – 399. Man in fancy dress, *c.* 1715.

400. Man's costume, c. 1720. – 401. Female dress, c. 1720. – 402. Little girls dressed like grown-up women; the dress of the bigger girl laced at the back, c. 1720. – 403. Lute player, c. 1720. – 404. Woman with bun worn high on head and loose-fitting gown (*contouche*), c. 1720. – 405. Woman wearing low-cut dress with tight-fitting stiffened bodice and hoop petticoat (*panier*); lace ruffle round neck, 1718. – 406. Man's dress, influenced by theatre, c. 1720.

407   408   409

ROCOCO
c. 1730–1770

410   411

407. Man wearing open coat (*justaucorps*), waistcoat of same length, lace-fronted shirt, lace cravat, knee-breeches (*culotte*), buckled shoes and three-cornered hat, *c.* 1725. – 408. Woman wearing loose gown (*contouche*) over hoop petticoat (*panier*), with frills (*engageantes*) at elbow and high-heeled shoes, *c.* 1725. – 409. Woman wearing gown (*contouche*) and small cap, *c.* 1715. – 410. Female dress with deep pleats in back ('Watteau pleats'), 1731. – 411. Children's dresses and woman in gown (*contouche*), *c.* 1730.

412. Peasant girl, *c.* 1730. – 413. Boy's dress with coat (*justaucorps*), skirt of which is lined with stiff material, 1739. – 414. Woman wearing apron and cap, 1739. – 415. Male dress: narrow shoulders with stiff, flared skirt, powdered wig with hair at back gathered into a bag tied with a bow (*crapaud*) from which a ribbon (*solitaire*) goes round neck, 1745. – 416. Girl's dress, 1745. – 417. Hunting costume, *c.* 1740.

418. Noblewoman in hunting costume worn over dome-shaped hoop petticoat (*panier*), with white-powdered hair, *c.* 1735. – 419–21. Male costume, *c.* 1770. – 422. Young girl with white-powdered hair, *c.* 1756. – 423. Woman with white-powdered hair, dressing cape, low-cut bodice with bows arranged in row (*échelle*), 1756. – 424. Man wearing powdered wig with side curls, hair at back gathered in a bag; silk dressing-gown over lace-trimmed shirt and knee-breeches fitting over stockings; buckled shoes, 1756.

425. Mme Pompadour in low-cut dress consisting of gown (robe), stomacher trimmed with bows, skirt (jupe) with deep flounce and trimming of artificial flowers; lace ruffle round neck, high-heeled shoes, 1738. – 426. Louis XV in coronation robes, c. 1730. – 427. Hunting costume, 1750. – 428. Peasant boy in sleeveless jacket (carmagnol), c. 1735. – 429. Woman wearing flat straw hat over powdered hair, low-cut dress consisting of gown (robe) and skirt (jupe), frills (engageantes) at elbow, stockings with garters and high-heeled slippers, 1766.

LOUIS XVI
c. 1770–1795

430. Woman with extravagant coiffure, calf-length skirt (*jupe*) and jacket with back pleats (*caraco*); in her hand a walking stick, 1778. – 431. Male costume, 1778. – 432. Woman wearing tulle cap on top of elaborate coiffure, gown (*robe*) looped up *à la polonaise*, 1778. – 433. Man wearing coat with skirt cut away towards back; powdered wig and buckled shoes, 1778. – 434. Woman wearing tulle cap over elaborate coiffure, calf-length skirt (*jupe*), and gown (*robe*) looped *à la polonaise*; in one hand a fan, in the other a parasol, 1778. – 435. Girls' dresses, 1778. – 436. Man wearing silk dressing gown, 1778.

437. Grey-powdered hair, stripes on both coat and stockings, 1788. – 438. Bustle (*cul de crin*) and fichu, 1788. – 439. Hat brim turned up front and back *à l'androsmane*, stripes on both coat and stockings, 1788. – 440. White dress, striped coat, fichu and large muff, 1788. – 441. Large straw hat with high crown and ostrich feathers, grey powdered hair, 1788. – 442. Coat made from woollen cloth instead of silk, grey-powdered hair, 1788. – 443. Muff, blue coat, yellow leather breeches, long black boots and beaver hat, 1789. – 444. Man's coat (*redingote*) over white dress, fichu and man's hat, 1789.

445. Short-waisted, double-breasted red coat, waistcoat cut square, two watch chains, 1790. –
446. Striped dress and high-crowned straw hat with ostrich feather, 1790. – 447. Long coat of
pink satin over white dress, 1791. – 448. High, turned-down collar and revers on both overcoat and
coat, 1791. – 449. Loose, unpowdered hair worn straight, 1792. – 450. 'Werther costume': blue
cloth coat with high turned-down collar, yellow leather breeches, riding boots and beaver hat,
1792. – 451. Cravat rising to chin, 1792. – 452. Fichu rising to chin, 1793.

453. All blue male costume with shoulder sash in red, white and blue, 1790. – 454. Dark blue masculine woman's dress with red lapels and cravat, hat with cockade and ostrich feathers, 1790. – 455. White dress, jacket laced in front; in the hand, a yo-yo, 1791. – 456. Grey-powdered hair with wreath of roses, red ribbon round neck, *à la guillotine*, 1791. – 457. Grey-powdered hair, brown coat with high red collar, yellow knee-breeches, blue embroidered waistcoat, 1791. – 458. Grey-powdered curled hair, small frilled hat, dress with stripes at hem, fichu, 1792. – 459. Grey-powdered hair, straw hat with ribbon under chin, fichu and scarf, 1792.

DIRECTOIRE

c. 1795–1804

460. *Merveilleuse*. Chemise gown with train, stockings with clocks, flat shoes, shawl and bonnet, 1796. – 461. *Incroyable*. Coat with wide lapels and turned-down collar, short waistcoat (*gilet*), tight trousers in boots, high neckcloth (*cravate*), hat with cockade, unkempt hair, and knotty stick, 1796. – 462. *Merveilleuse*, 1796. – 463. 'Greek' dress worn by Mme Tallien, 1797. – 464. Coat with wide lapels and turned-down collar, tight breeches, short waistcoat, and large cravat, 1796. – 465. Chemise gown and sandals, 1796. – 466. Greek coiffure, chemise gown and sandals, 1796. – 467. Coat, tight breeches, high cravat, and top boots, 1796.

468. Chemise gown, shawl, and ostrich feather in hair, 1800. – 469. Skater wearing chemise gown and long gloves, 1800. – 470. Skater wearing long, tight trousers (pantaloons), coat and top hat, 1800. – 471. Skater wearing tight pantaloons and short jacket, 1800. – 472. Man wearing coat with high, double collar and narrow tails; cocked hat, 1801. – 473. Turban, tunic over chemise gown with train, 1801. – 474. Chemise gown with velvet train falling from sleeveless waistcoat, 1801. – 475. Same dress from behind; head-dress of ostrich feathers, 1801.

78

EMPIRE
c. 1804–1820

476. Dress with train and long sleeves, shawl, sash round waist, 1803. – 477. Velvet *redingote* with train, narrow sleeves and high waist-line, 1805. – 478. Dress with puffed sleeves and shawl, 1806. – 479. Light brown *redingote* seen from front, 1806. – 480. White dress with train, bonnet, long yellow gloves, green shawl over arm, 1806. – 481. Plain white ankle-length dress, very low-cut, with puffed sleeves; long white gloves, flat shoes, 1806. – 482. White dress, yellow gloves, yellow shawl, scarf rourd neck, 1806. – 483. Blue dress, white shawl, yellow gloves and jointed parasol, 1806.

484   485   486   487

488   489   490   491

484. Man wearing grey tail-coat, knee-breeches, riding boots, cravat and top hat, 1806. – 485. Long pale-blue coat trimmed with white fur, yellow shawl, 1807. – 486. White dress with pale blue appliqué work, white gloves, 1807. – 487. Man wearing brown spencer over blue tail-coat, yellow leather breeches, riding boots, 1807. – 488. White, ankle-length, low-cut dress, yellow gloves, red shawl, 1807. – 489. White dress, green shawl, 1807. – 490. Pink dress with serrated trimming (*dents de loup*), green fichu, green gloves, yellow shawl in hand, 1807. – 491. White dress with garland of flowers embroidered at hem, blue fichu, yellow gloves, red shawl in hand, 1807.

492. Pale blue dress, white apron with serrated edge; fichu, shoes with cross-lacing, 1807. – 493. Evening dress with high cravat and two waistcoats, 1807. – 494. White straw bonnet, white dress, green gloves and shawl, yellow fichu, 1807. – 495. White dress with long sleeves, white shoes, 1807. – 496. Velvet *redingote*, slashed sleeves reminiscent of German Renaissance costume, 1807. – 497. Coat (*redingote*) and small hat (*toque*), 1807. – 498. Dress frilled at hem, turban with *esprit*, 1808. – 499. Pink dress with appliqué work at hem, 1808.

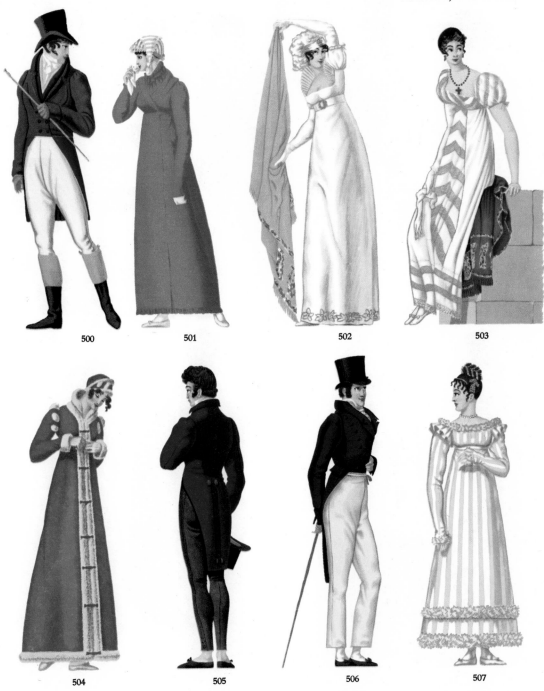

500. Green spencer jacket over blue tail-coat, yellow breeches, riding boots, top hat, 1808. – 501. Long, ankle-length *redingote*, 1808. – 502. Plain white dress, gloves, hat with ostrich feather, light brown shawl, 1808. – 503. Low-cut white dress with puffed sleeves, red shawl, 1808. – 504. Long green coat trimmed with fur, and small hat to match, 1809. – 505. Blue tail-coat, long narrow knitted pantaloons, white stockings and flat shoes, 1816. – 506. Wide, yellow nankeen trousers, blue tail-coat, short waistcoat, top hat and pumps, 1808. – 507. Ankle-length plain dress with long sleeves and horizontal neckline trimmed with ruching, high coiffure, 1816.

508. Poke bonnet and flat shoes, white dress with appliqué work, belt at natural waist-line, 1823. –
509. Man wearing top hat, long trousers with strap under instep, and waisted coat with sleeves full
at shoulder; side-whiskers, 1823. – 510. Tail-coat, knee-breeches, curly hair, side-whiskers, 1824. –
511. White dress with oval neckline, high asymmetrically dressed hair with ringlets at temples,
1824. – 512. Man wearing waisted overcoat with cape; top hat, 1824. – 513. Coat with cape and
falling collar; bag in hand (*reticule*) introduced in Directoire period, 1823. – 514. Couple in evening
dress, both wearing cloaks with shoulder-capes, 1824.

515. Riding costume: tight white breeches, green tail-coat wide at shoulders, boots with spurs, and beaver hat, 1825. – 516. Bonnet, dress with appliqué work *à la grecque*, shawl, 1825. – 517. Dress with *broderie anglaise* trimming, shawl over arm, 1825. – 518. Man wearing court dress, 1825. – 519. Dress with leg-of-mutton sleeves, falling collar and appliqué work, 1825. – 520. Embroidered collar, leg-of-mutton sleeves, hair dressed asymmetrically with ringlets, 1825. – 521. Dress with appliqué work and leg-of-mutton sleeves, flat shoes, large bonnet; 1825. – 522. Top hat, waisted cloth coat, velvet trousers, two waistcoats, one over the other, 1825.

523. Hour-glass silhouette. Wasp waist, plain wide skirt over several petticoats, sleeves widest at elbows, shoulders very sloping, 1832. – 524. Little girl in pantalets, 1832. – 525. Top hat and mauve waisted coat, tight grey trousers with strap under instep, 1832. – 526. Little girl with pantalets gathered in at ankle, 1832. – 527. Boy in top hat, long trousers, and waisted coat with wide sleeves, 1832. – 528. Top hat and waisted coat, 1833. – 529. Riding habit with sleeves joined below shoulders, 1833. – 530. Hour-glass silhouette; blue spotted dress, bonnet, and flat shoes with cross-bands, 1832. – 531. Long, waisted coat with shawl collar, 1833.

532. Indoor costume: woman with smooth hair parted in middle, pinafore over dress with horizontal décolletage and filled in by scarf; man's suit of grey cashmere with red silk sash, 1834. – 533. Riding dress with train and hat with ostrich feathers, 1834. – 534. Informal man's costume: long white trousers with strap under instep, tail-coat and silk top hat, 1834. – 535. Children's dresses. The girl wears pantalets, the boy a skirted blouse, 1834. – 536. Boys' costumes, 1834. – 537. Shooting costume, 1834.

538. Evening dress with evening cloak over mauve tail-coat, white waistcoat, and long white trousers, 1837. – 539. Evening dress with evening cloak for young man, 1837. – 540. Little girl in embroidered muslin dress with pigtail, 1837. – 541. Bonnet with marabou feather, organdie dress with off-the-shoulder neckline, and shawl, 1837. – 542. Bonnet and parasol, batiste dress with frills, V-shaped neckline, 1837. – 543. Visiting costume: reddish-brown waisted coat, long grey trousers and top hat, 1839. – 544. Court dress, 1837. – 545. Evening dress in black and white, 1837.

546   547   548   549

550   551   552   553

546. Silk-lined waisted coat, brown tail-coat, long black trousers, white cravat, top hat, 1836. – 547. Bonnet of silk, coat of brocade, 1836. – 548. Bonnet, coat with slits for arms, 1836. – 549. Man in walking costume: blue waisted coat, grey striped trousers, yellow waistcoat, top hat, 1836. – 550. Wedding dress of white lace, 1837. – 551. Summer dress, large bonnet with veil, 1837. – 552. Visiting dress: off-the-shoulder neckline, tight lacing, long skirts, large bonnet, 1837. – 553. Indoor costume: dress with off-the-shoulder neckline, pinafore, plaits at the ears, 1837.

554. Dress with off-the-shoulder neckline and bell-shaped skirt, shawl and ringlets, 1840. – 555. Waisted coat, long trousers and top hat, 1840. – 556. Boy's costume with long trousers, 1840. – 557. Girl with hair combed straight, covering ears; dress with full skirts and pantalets, 1840. – 558. Striped waisted coat, long white trousers, and top hat, 1840. – 559. Long narrow sleeves, corseted waist, bell-shaped skirt, straight hair covering ears, 1840. – 560. Hunting habit with pantalets, 1840. – 561. Hunting costume, similar to that worn today, 1840.

562. Bonnet, black silk coat shorter than dress, 1844. – 563. Green waisted coat, trousers with oblique stripes, top hat, 1841. – 564. Bonnet with veil, claret-coloured silk coat shorter than dress, 1844. – 565. White bonnet, blue-and-white striped silk skirt, skirted jacket, 1945. – 566. Riding habit with long skirt, tight-fitting jacket, top hat with veil, 1846. – 567. Bonnet, dress with tight pointed bodice overlapping skirt, which is flounced, 1846.

568. Green crinoline dress with white undersleeves attached, small green bonnet, 1849. – 569. Child's dress: hat with ostrich feather, coat with cape, gaiters, 1847. – 570. Bonnet and crinoline dress with narrow sleeves, 1847. – 571. Man's costume in blue with check trousers, 1847. – 572. Short coat with hood, over crinoline dress, 1848. – 573. Bonnet and black shawl trimmed with lace over crinoline dress, 1848. – 574. White bonnet, black shawl over crinoline dress, 1848. – 575. Bonnet and triangular shawl over crinoline dress, 1848.

576   577   578   579

580   581   582   583

576. Bonnet and velvet crinoline dress with white lace collar and cuffs, 1847. – 577. Flounced ball gown; flowers in hair, and on breast, shoulders and skirt, 1847. – 578. Scarlet velvet jacket over grey, braided crinoline dress, 1848. – 579. Green dressing-gown with quilted pink lining, 1848. – 580. Bonnet and coat with cape, white collar, white gloves, and white handkerchief, 1848. – 581. Boy in long trousers, black cape and bowler hat; girl in long pantalets and buttoned boots, 1848. – 582. Ball gown; round shoulders, a *bertha* with frill matching five flounces on skirt, 1847. – 583. Ball gown with tassels on skirt, bodice and hair; short gloves, 1847.

584   585   586   587

588   589   590

584. Man wearing short overcoat and top hat, 1849. – 585. Man wearing striped trousers, frock coat, check waistcoat, necktie, and top hat, 1857. – 586. Man wearing short overcoat with loose hanging sleeves, 1857. – 587. Man wearing top hat and cloak, 1856. – 588. Mother in lace bonnet and crinoline dress, child in white embroidered christening robe such as is still used, 1851. – 589. Bonnet and short coat over crinoline dress, 1851. – 590. *Capote* hat tied under chin, crinoline dress with funnel-shaped sleeves and white undersleeves, 1855.

591   592   593   594

595   596   597   598

591. Check trousers, short loose sports coat trimmed with astrakhan, bowler, 1866. – 592. Blue overcoat trimmed with astrakhan, striped trousers, top hat, 1866. – 593. Yellow suit, short overcoat, necktie, and bowler, 1862. – 594. Light suit, light overcoat, bowler, 1862. – 595. Little girl in wide-skirted dress, mittens and cloth boots, 1857. – 596. Crinoline dress, with funnel-shaped sleeves and white undersleeves, parasol, 1857. – 597. Crinoline dress with five flounces on skirt, tight high-necked bodice with *pagoda* sleeves showing three flounces and displaying white, attached undersleeves; *capote* hat tied under chin, 1857. – 598. Crinoline replaced by looped-up skirt, 1870.

599   600   601   602

603   604   605   606

599. Morning coat, striped trousers and top hat, 1881. – 600. Dress of two kinds of material with bustle; high collar, tight sleeves, emphasis on bust and abdomen; drapery swinging low in front, looped up at back, 1882. – 601. Bustle dress with train, high-heeled boots, 1882. – 602. Bustle dress seen from side, 1882. – 603. Bustle dress with skirt caught up at sides, 1882. – 604. Boys' suits with short tight breeches and boots, 1882. – 605. Light summer suit and flat straw hat, 1882. – 606. Bustle dress, flowered skirt falling loose, coat with very full skirt, high *capote* hat, 1882.

607. Bustle dress with loose-falling skirt draped up at back, 1885. – 608. Bustle dress caught up at sides, 1885 – 609. Bustle dress and waisted jacket. Boy's suit with baggy knee-breeches, 1888. – 610. Overcoat, check trousers and top hat, 1888. – 611. Bustle dress as skating costume, 1888. – 612. Check sports suit with short tight breeches and fur cap, 1888. – 613. Evening gown without bustle, 1890. – 614. The bustle has disappeared, but the dress is still looped up, 1890.

615. Long-waisted dress with faint trace of looping up, puffed sleeves, flat straw hat, 1890. – 616. Tailor-made costume with high shoulders, 1891. – 617. Evening gown with leg-of-mutton sleeves and train, 1894. – 618. High-necked evening gown with large sleeves, 1895. – 619. Hour-glass figure and leg-of-mutton sleeves, 1895. – 620. Summer dress fitting closely over corseted figure, 1898. – 621. Green dress with trumpet-shaped skirt, sway-back carriage, 1899. – 622. High-necked dress with trumpet-shaped skirt, sway-back carriage, 1900.

THE TWENTIETH CENTURY *c.* 1900–1910 97

623. The 'fine figure' emphasized by dress being draped in spirals round body, 1902. – 624. Dress with blouse-shaped bodice and high collar; sway-back, 1903. – 625. Big hat, high coiffure and boa; sway-back, 1905. – 626. Check *paletot*, narrow trousers and bowler, 1905. – 627. Evening gown and hair pad, 1907. – 628. Big hat with feathers; sway-back, 1908. – 629. Big hat; sway-back, 1909. – 630. Big hat, hobble skirt, rectangular muff, 1910.

631. The 'fish silhouette.' Narrow evening dress with train and large muff, by Bourniche, 1912. – 632. Evening wrap shaped like Japanese kimono, by Laferrière, 1912. – 633. Evening wrap draped like Japanese kimono, by Paquin, 1912. – 634. Semi-crinoline coat with high waist, bodice and sleeves cut in one, over long pleated skirt, by Poiret, 1913. – 635. Sports costume, 1913. – 636. Fish silhouette. Dinner gown with sleeves and bodice cut in one, high waist and draped skirt, 1913. – 637. Coat with scarf, and belt threaded through, by Poiret, 1917. – 638. Summer dress mid-calf length, sleeves and bodice cut in one, 1920.

639. Mourning dress with wide belt round hips, 1922. – 640. Costume reaching just below knee, 1923. – 641. Knee-length dress of gold lamé with coat to match, by Patou, 1925. – 642. Fur coat, 1925. – 643. Evening dress of georgette, sleeveless, with belt round hips, by Patou, 1926. – 644. Suit with pointed lapels and turn-up on trousers, 1920. – 645. Straight dress and Eton crop, 1927. – 646. Sleeveless dress with belt round hips. Eton crop, 1928. – 647. Knee-length costume and cloche hat, 1928.

648. Long, backless evening gown, by Patou. Material cut bias, 1935. – 649. Long, backless evening gown, by Patou, 1935. – 650. Costume suit with coat, by Schiaparelli, 1936. – 651. Costume suit with coat, by Mainbocher, 1936. – 652. *Redingote*, by Alix, 1936. – 653. Backless evening gown, by Alix. Hair dressed high on head, 1938. – 654. Evening gown and cape, by Lanvin. Hair dressed high on head, 1938. – 655. Elegant lounging pyjamas, by Schiaparelli, 1937.

656. Top hat, tail coat, 1943. – 657. Strapless evening gown, by Paquin, 1946. – 658. Cape over long evening dress, by Schiaparelli, 1947. – 659. Dress with V-neckline and elbow-length sleeves, 1948. – 660. New Look: longer and wider dresses, 1948. – 661. New Look: ankle-length coat, very wide skirt, 1948. – 662. Loose swagger jacket over narrow skirt, hat with scarf over ears, 1948. – 663. Swagger coat over narrow skirt, small hat with veil, 1948. – 664. Dress with cuffs at shoulders, small hat, 1950. – 665. Suit with close-fitting slit skirt, and beret, 1950.

666   667   668   669   670

671   672   673   674

666. Long strapless evening gown, train attached, 1952. – 667. Little girl in sun suit; horse's tail coiffure, 1953. – 668. Short evening gown of lace with V-neckline, ankle-strap shoes, 1952. – 669. Suit and fur stole, 1953. – 670. Lounge suit, trilby hat, shirt with soft collar, thick-soled shoes, 1952. – 671. Slacks, sweater, and swagger coat, 1953. – 672. Jeans, stole round shoulders, basket instead of bag, hair short and combed upwards at back, 1953. – 673. Striped skirt, wide elastic belt, small scarf round neck, 1954. – 674. Lounge suit, 1954.

675. Hem well below knee, bust emphasized, 1956. – 676. ‹Sack' dress with ‹hobble' hem-line, 1957. – 677. Conventional male costume, discreet colours, 1957. – 678. Trapeze line, 1957. – 679. Rising hem, tall boots, bust de-emphasized 1963. – 680. Long evening gown, psychedelic patterns, 1966. – 681. Tent-shaped evening gown, flowing lines, 1966.

682. Female trouser suit, 1967. – 683. Miniskirted 'little girl dress', chain necklace, tall boots, 1967. – 684. The Beatles: bright colours, romantic styling, long hair, 1967. – 685. One-piece trouser suit for formal wear, psychedelic patterns, 1968. – 686. Female trouser suit inspired by India. – 687. Changes in traditional male costume: disappearance of collar and tie, 1968. – 688. Miniskirted dress with coat from the same material, psychedelic patterns, 1968. – 689. Maxi-coat over miniskirt, renewed emphasis on female figure, 1970.

COSTUME CAVALCADE

Egypt

c. 3000–500 B.C.

(*Figs. 1–30*)

The earliest Western civilizations known to us arose along the Nile Valley in Egypt and on the plain lying between the Tigris and the Euphrates. Which preceded the other is an open question. Both flourished for several thousand years before the beginning of the Christian era, but more monuments of ancient civilization have survived in Egypt because the material used there for temples and pyramids was stone. They look as if they had been built to last for ever, and in fact many of them have remained more or less intact for thousands of years.

The Egyptian style is characterized by severity, regularity, order and rhythmical repetition. Rows of figures form avenues in front of the temples and also appear on the walls of tombs. Even the lotus of the Nile was incorporated in this rigid pattern. Egyptian columns take the shape of long stems surmounted by bunches of closed lotus flowers, or single open blossoms. A grooved band near the top of the pillar seems to help the frail stems to support the weight of the roof.

The wall paintings give us a clear idea of Egyptian dress. The figures were either rendered by outlines incised into the surface of the stone, or carved in flat relief and richly painted in bright colours, or, as became increasingly the practice, painted directly on to the wall.

Here we see the costume of ancient Egypt. Because of the warm climate it was much simpler than our own.

Egypt's first period of prosperity was the Old Kingdom (*c.* 2780–2280 B.C.) lasting from the third to the sixth dynasty. The masculine garment was then a short, plain loin-cloth of linen wrapped tightly round the hips and secured by a belt with a loop. It was retained throughout the period as a convenient and practical working dress. (*1–3.*)

The contemporary royal dress was also a loin-cloth, but not of linen. As far as can be seen from the paintings, it was woven with gold thread, and the peculiar arrangement of the folds in front remained part of the royal dress even after it had come to consist of several garments (*12, 23*).

The feminine dress of the Old Kingdom, like the earliest masculine dress, was a single garment. This was a long, plain, close-fitting skirt covering the body from under the breasts to the ankles and supported by one or two shoulder straps. It persisted alongside later types of dress in subsequent periods (*7, 10, 18, 22, 24*).

The fourth and fifth dynasties were the period of the great pyramids. The short, tight loin-cloth of the masculine dress then became wider, and the linen was starched. The wall paintings show it as a small pyramid hanging from the waist, a fashion which was retained in the royal dress (*9*).

Egypt's next period of prosperity was from the eleventh to the thirteenth dynasties, the Middle Kingdom (*c.* 2065–1660 B.C.). Men's dress was no longer a single loin-cloth but several skirts, one above the other. Underneath was the short loin-cloth, with over it a longer one reaching nearly to the ankles (*4*).

Women's dress of the Middle Kingdom shows no change from the previous period. The long, close-fitting skirt was the only garment, giving the figure the appearance of a slender obelisk.

After a period of disruption caused by foreign raids the country settled down to a third period of prosperity during the eighteenth to twenty-first dynasties, or New Kingdom (*c.* 1580–950 B.C.). Both men's and women's dress underwent a radical transformation, for with the conquest of Syria the Asiatic seamed tunic (*28*) or *kalasiris* became part of the Egyptian costume. Men wore it with the one or more skirts of the preceding

period, the tunic going either over or under them
(*5, 6, 10, 11*). For women it became the principal
garment and was supplemented with a cape knotted on the breast (*12, 13, 16, 20, 21*). One would
expect these two garments to conceal more of the
body than the single skirt, which did not cover the
breasts, but the linen was so fine in texture that it
revealed the naked body as through a veil. In this
elaborate costume of thin, transparent linen, pleating appeared for the first time, both in the masculine (*11, 19*), and the feminine (*20, 21*) garment.
The stylized folds of the pleated dress fell into a
pattern of fine lines which followed the shape of
the drapery, and the material, made heavier and
more fluid by the pleating, clung lightly to the
body with none of the severity of the earlier costume. These pleated dresses were especially characteristic of the twenty years or so of the New
Kingdom which we now call the Amarna period.
During his short reign from 1370–1352 B.C. the
heretical King Akhenaten (Amenhotep IV) moved
the capital of the country from Thebes to Amarna,
where he tried to replace the traditional pantheism
of the priests by the worship of the sun as the only
god. The King and his beautiful Queen Nefertiti
wore this finely pleated dress (*21*), the graceful

White crown of Upper Egypt

arrangement of which emphasizes the degenerate
grace of their bodies. Their skulls were of a peculiar pear shape (*17*), possibly as a result of artificial
deformation similar to that practised today by
certain negro tribes in Central Africa.

The Egyptians are depicted as being bare-
footed; only kings and priests wore sandals (*12,
19, 23*). A ceremonial leopard skin (*19*) formed

part of the costume of the priests, and the kings
wore either the combined red crown of Lower
Egypt and white crown of Upper Egypt or the
cap-shaped crown bearing the emblem of a serpent (*12, 23*).

Red crown of Lower Egypt. Royal skirt

Towards the end of the New Kingdom the exquisite art of dressmaking in the Amarna period
began to decline. Garments were more brightly
coloured, pleating disappeared, and the linen was
plain and slightly starched. The influence of Asia
is apparent in the completely un-Egyptian fashion
of finishing the material in fringes.

Flowers (*8, 10, 15, 20*) and jewellery were extensively used as decoration. Faience beads and semi-
precious stones such as lapis lazuli and cornelian
were set in gold to make bracelets, diadems and
girdles (*14*). The most typical ornament, however,
was the large shoulder-cape, the vivid colours and
circular shape of which made it a very important
part of the costume (*11, 12, 18, 19, 22*).

The Egyptians also developed an elaborate
beauty culture which included the use of cosmetics.
A cone of ointment mixed with perfume was
placed in the hair, where it slowly melted and
spread its fragrance (*7, 8, 13, 15, 20*), and the body
was rubbed with sweet-smelling oils. The eye-
brows were pencilled with black, and green eye-
shadow was used. The men were beardless, although on ceremonial occasions the king wore a
false beard (*9*). Wigs of wool or false hair were
also used. Towards the end of the New Kingdom
it was fashionable for women to wear large wigs
which gave their heads a squarish appearance (*10,
14, 21*).

In surveying the long history of Egyptian costume, it would be true to say that on the whole it did not undergo any great modification. The reason for this is that with the Egyptians a respect for tradition was stronger than the need for change. It is this attitude which makes both Egyptian art and Egyptian costume seem so strikingly conservative.

The Neighbouring Peoples

Pictures of neighbouring peoples are often found in Egyptian tomb paintings, and a few examples have been included here to show how their costume compares with that of the Egyptians. The illustration of the Syrian archer shows the Asiatic dress which, as the *kalasiris* (28), became part of Egyptian costume during the New Kingdom. Here it is worn either alone or with drapery wound in a spiral round the body (29, 30), the latter being the characteristic garment of the country between the Euphrates and the Tigris which we now call Mesopotamia. There are also pictures of a Semitic people whose women wear tunics covering the left shoulder (26). The material is not the linen of Egypt, which was either white or dyed in a single colour, but wool woven in a close pattern. Wool—also with a pattern—is again used in the loin-cloth of a Semitic shepherd whose sandals are of an entirely different design from the flat sandals of the Egyptians (25). The illustrations also show a patterned loin-cloth worn by a Syrian ambassador (27) the lower front of which is weighted—a type of loin-cloth which reappears later in the masculine dress of Crete and Mycenae.

The costumes of all these neighbouring peoples were quite unlike those worn in Egypt, and each difference of detail has been accurately depicted. But the figures themselves conform to the Egyptian ideal, for the artists gave them the conventional outlines of Egyptians, with broad shoulders, narrow hips, and straight legs.

The contrast between the two kinds of costume emphasizes both the distinctive style of Egyptian dress and the fact that it changed very little throughout the thousand years of the country's history.

The Aegean

c. 2000–1100 B.C.

(*Figs. 31–37*)

In Egyptian tomb paintings foreign peoples and their ambassadors are shown bringing rich gifts to the ruler of Egypt. During the reign of Thutmosis III and in the succeeding Amarna period a new race made its appearance among these ambassadors, the long-legged people from *Kftiu* and the 'islands of the sea'. Egyptian dress subsequently took on a freer, more decorative aspect, perhaps under the influence of the Mediterranean islands to the north.

Until the end of the nineteenth century little was known of the people from *Kftiu*, which was the *Kaphtor* of the Bible and the Crete of our own time. In about 1870, however, Heinrich Schliemann began his excavations on the site of Troy, the city of the Iliad near the Dardanelles, and later proceeded to excavate the fortresses of Tiryns and Mycenae on the Greek mainland. Later, Sir Arthur Evans uncovered the palace at Cnossos and other royal residences in Crete. These discoveries have given us a detailed knowledge of the brilliant, Bronze Age civilization of Crete and Mycenae

Cretan seen by an Egyptian artist

which existed centuries before that of the Greeks. Crete, the island in the middle of the sea, equidistant from Asia, Egypt and the Greek mainland, was the natural centre for trade, and this civilization flourished there from about 2000 to 1400 B.C., and from 1600 to 1100 B.C. at Tiryns and Mycenae on the Greek mainland. It was overthrown and entirely destroyed by the Dorian migrations of about 1000 B.C. when the Greeks, armed with the new victorious metal, iron, occupied the Aegean islands.

Whereas the typical Egyptian of the tomb paintings was slender, with a somewhat stiff carriage, broad shoulders, straight legs and narrow hips, the typical Cretan combined slimness with rounded curves. The illustrations show how the long, supple limbs, the slender waist and the pronounced backward tilt of the upper part of the body are all emphasized by the costume.

As in ancient Egypt, the masculine costume in Crete was a short loin-cloth. The Syrian tunic appears occasionally (31), but only as a foreign importation. The Cretan loin-cloth, however, produced quite a different effect from the Egyptian; it was weighted at the lower front corner, sometimes by a net of pearls (36), while the loin-cloth itself was fastened higher on the waist and secured by a wide belt, possibly of leather, with padded edges, which acted as a corset, producing a wasp-waist and making the hips appear rounder and fuller (32, 36). The same corseting effect is apparent even if the skirt consists only of separate cloths back and front—the so-called 'half-skirt', which left the hips bare (35).

As well as being the masculine costume, the half-skirt was also part of the dress worn by the Cretan goddess holding serpents in her upraised hands (37). She is thought to be of Babylonian origin, and the idea represented is possibly the same as in the story of Eve and the serpent in the Bible.

Women's dress in Crete is known both from votive figures (37) and from frescoes. It is a two-piece costume consisting of a bell-shaped, tiered skirt and a small jacket, the skirt with a pattern of bright colours running in alternate squares and stripes over the tiers. As far as can be seen from the pictures, the tiers were either flounces or were produced by several skirts of decreasing length worn one over the other. The fullness of the skirt increased the width of the hips, while the waist was reduced by the same tight, wide, padded belt as was worn by the men. It is most surprising that the women wearing this long, full skirt, which completely hides the lower part of the body and the legs, have the breasts exposed. The jacket consists only of back and sleeves, and displays the breasts in all their exuberant nakedness. Both men and women wore their hair over the forehead in loose twined curls which repeated the characteristic motif of Cretan art—the supple, vigorous line of the spiral.

The inhabitants of the Greek mainland during the Mycenaean period may have been a different race from the Cretans, but the women wore Cretan dress (34). This, incidentally, illustrates one of the difficulties of interpreting costume. In the frescoes the full, tiered skirt is shown as ending in two curved lines at the hem, and for this reason it has sometimes been described as a trouser-skirt in which each leg was thought to be made up of separate tiers or flounces. This is erroneous. The curved lines are an attempt by the artist to render as clearly as possible the billowing width of the skirt and to give at the same time an impression of the many layers of material which composed it.

The dress for men on the Greek mainland was not the Cretan loin-cloth but a short *chiton* hanging from the shoulders (33). This later became an important garment in Greek costume.

Cretan spiral pattern

Scandinavia

c. 1500–1200 B.C.

Danish costume in the Bronze Age

Our knowledge of Egyptian and Cretan costume is derived from wall paintings or sculptural reliefs and statues. But contemporaneous with the civilization of Crete and Mycenae in the Aegean was the Scandinavian Bronze Age, which began in about 1500 B.C. By a remarkable chance, costumes from this period have been preserved up to the present time, but as there are no contemporary pictorial representations of them they have not been reproduced among the coloured illustrations in this book.

In the Early Bronze Age it was the practice in Scandinavia to bury the bodies of persons of the upper class in coffins made of hollowed oak trunks split in two so that the halves when placed together fitted very closely. Over the coffin was piled a grave-mound of earth. The acid of the oak together with the covering of earth have preserved both the coffin and the clothing worn by the body when it was buried, and these dresses of more than 3,000 years ago can still be seen in the National Museum of Copenhagen. One can examine the weaving, measure the garments, and get a fairly accurate idea of how they must have been worn from their position in the coffin.

These oak coffin finds have given us seven complete costumes: four male (from the graves at Borum Aeshøj, Trindhøj, and Muldbjerg), and three female (from the graves at Borum Aeshøj, Egtved and Skrydstrup).

The man's costume consists of cap, shoes, cloak and under-garment, the material having been woven from sheep's wool in a twill weave. The cap is either a skull-cap or a tall cap, the crown and sides of which were made separately; the cloak is oval or kidney-shaped and is turned out at the neck to form a sort of shawl collar; the shoes are of leather, and were probably worn over a foot-wrapping of cloth. Like the cloak, the undergarment consists of a length of material without seams, forming either a loin-cloth, like those of the two male costumes from Borum Aeshøj, or long enough to reach above the chest. In the latter, the two upper corners had been lengthened for attachment to leather shoulder straps. This garment is known from the examples found at Trindhøj and Muldbjerg, and was worn in conjunction with the large kidney-shaped cloak. Both the cloak and a round cap from Trindhøj were covered with a short pile which was possibly intended to imitate the hairy coat of an animal.

Man's costume from Muldbjerg

The three women's costumes were all in two pieces, one garment falling from the shoulders, the other from the hips. The upper garment, which is identical in all three, is a short closed blouse with short sleeves and a horizontal slit for the head. It is made of a rectangular piece of material joined at the back with a T-shaped seam which is continued down the sleeve under the arm.

Two of the women's costumes (Borum Aeshøj and Skrydstrup) include a piece of material shaped like a skirt and carelessly sewn together. We do not know how the woman of Borum Aeshøj wore it as the excavation was not undertaken by experts, but with the woman from Skrydstrup it was draped round the lower part of the body and legs in large folds like a skirt. Because of its great length and width and the casual way in which the vertical seam has been sewn, the experts think it was probably not worn as a skirt by a living woman but was used only as a shroud. This does not, however, exclude the possibility that the blouse may have been worn with a long woven skirt.

A third feminine costume from Egtved has actually given us a real skirt, although a very peculiar one, for it is short, resting on the hips and scarcely coming down to the knees. It is not sewn together, but was wrapped twice round the body; nor is it woven like the other garments, but is of

Woman's costume from Egtved

cords forming a wide fringe and held together by a woven edge at the top and by a plaited cord at the bottom. When wrapped round the body, this thick fringe formed a garment covering the body from hip to knee. The blouse hung from the shoulders. A woven belt with a round belt-plate of bronze was, as far as can be judged from its position in the coffin, fastened round the naked waist. The feminine costume also included leather shoes and foot-wrappings.

That the braided skirt was in fact a skirt, and that it was actually worn in the early Bronze Age, is confirmed by some small bronze figures of the period in which it is the only garment.

The feminine costume of the Scandinavian

Bronze Age consisted, then, of two parts: the blouse, which hung from the shoulders, and the skirt, which hung from the hips.

Of all the feminine costumes known to us from antiquity, the only one at all resembling the Scandinavian costume is that from Crete, with its jacket and tiered skirt.

Denmark is a long way from the Mediterranean, and in ancient times the distance must have been immense. It may seem a rash assumption to regard the existence of two-piece costumes in both areas as anything more than a coincidence, but the characteristic techniques of a civilization, as they appear in the shape of its utensils or the cut of its clothes, can travel far if given time. A folding chair found in the Guldhøj grave has its counterpart in Egypt; a shawl from the Trindhøj grave is the only woven garment finished with the fringe characteristic of the Mesopotamians of antiquity.

The most typical ornamental design of Crete, the spiral, reappears in the decorative work of the

Scandinavian spiral pattern   *Figure with cord skirt*

Danish Bronze Age, e.g. in the round belt-plates. The metal itself, bronze, reached Scandinavia from the outside world, just as the golden amber of the North found its way to the shores of the Mediterranean. Is it quite beyond the bounds of possibility that the fashion of the two-piece feminine costume may in turn have travelled north?

Greece

c. 700–150 B.C.

(Figs. 38–73)

The Greek immigrants came in several waves, and their arrival meant the end of the Cretan-Mycenaean civilization. First they captured and burned the Cretan palaces, the open halls of which were unfortified because up till then the encircling

sea had given them sufficient protection. They next took the fortresses on the Greek mainland, in spite of their massive defences. This brilliant civilization was soon only a memory, to be handed down to future generations in the epic poems of Homer.

Between 1200 and 1000 B.C. the Greek tribes moved into their future homeland, the first to arrive being the Ionians, followed by the Achaeans, and lastly by the Dorians. Of these the Dorians were the strongest, and they succeeded in driving the Ionians across the sea to the west coast of Asia Minor, which, as Ionia, thus became part of ancient Greece.

The first historical period of Greece, called the 'archaic', lasted from about 700 to 475 B.C., that is, until just after the Persian Wars. No information about its costume is available until about 600 B.C., when the Greeks began to make 'black-figured' vases, in which the design was executed in black on the reddish-brown surface of the clay. These stiff, rather elongated figures display the various types of early Greek costume.

Men wore either the short *chiton*, a close-fitting garment of tunic form (*40*), or the long, smooth, ceremonial *chiton*, often with a pattern (*38, 41*). These garments, of which the former had already appeared in the Cretan-Mycenaean period (cf. *33*), were the usual dress of the tribes inhabiting Greece itself, but during the same period a long, pleated, linen *chiton* was worn in Ionia and from there crossed the sea to the Greek mainland (*43, 46*).

The masculine costume included a cloak, worn either as the sole garment or over the *chiton*. There were two kinds of cloaks: a smaller one, folded double over the shoulders (*38, 39, 41*), and the large, loosely draped *himation* (*43, 45*, and cf. *48, 52, 53*), which was retained throughout the period.

Closed peplos

The feminine costume, as shown on the black-figured vases, was the *peplos*, a long, woollen, tunic-like garment with a high, belted waist. It was tubular in shape, and a little longer than the body. The tube was formed of a rectangular piece of woollen material with the two vertical edges seamed together; the top edge was folded out-

wards at shoulder level, and the front and back were fastened together with two pins, with the back over-lapping the front. The pins thus passed through four thicknesses of material, which prevented the soft wool from being torn. These fastenings left three openings at the top of the tube, the head going through the middle one, the arms through the other two. Because the upper part was folded outwards to fall over the breast, the material here was of double thickness, giving the 'overfold' or *apoptygma*, the distinctive feature of the *peplos* (*42, 44*).

Towards the end of the period, from about 550 to 480 B.C., the influence of Ionia began to increase. Our knowledge of Greek costume now comes from the 'red-figured' vases, in which the design in light colours was painted on a black background, and which superseded the black-figured vases in about 530 B.C. Light pleated linen now replaced wool, and Herodotus mentions that during this period the feminine costume changed from the old-fashioned woollen *peplos* to the Ionic linen *chiton*. Like the *peplos*, the *chiton* was a tubular garment fastened at the shoulders, but there were a number of differences between them. Since the material was pleated, the *chiton* was much wider, and as it consisted of two widths of material instead of one, there was a seam running down either side. It was as long as the *peplos*, but instead of hanging in an overfold from the shoulders, the extra material was pulled up over the belt, producing a blouse-like effect. This was called the

Chiton with 'false sleeves'

kolpos (*49, 57*) and was as much a part of the *chiton* as the overfold was of the *peplos*. Like the *peplos*, the *chiton* was fastened at the top with pins, but there were more of them because, as the pleating made it very wide, there was room for a row of pins or buttons on either side of the neck-opening. These fastenings along the shoulder and the upper arm, together with the fullness of the material, gave the costume the appearance of having sleeves (*49, 50, 58*), which, with the blouse-like fullness or *kolpos* supported by the belt, are the distinctive feature of the *chiton*.

The pleated linen *chiton* of the late archaic period is a very rich costume compared to the severe, closely fitting *peplos* which it supplanted, and it is hardly surprising that Solon tried to curb this luxury by legislation.

The cloak worn over the *chiton* was either the voluminous *himation*, similar to the masculine garment (*50, 57*), or a smaller one worn transversely. The latter was a narrow shawl folded into a band running from the right shoulder across the chest and under the left arm, then up over the back to the right shoulder again, from which the loose ends hung down in swallow-tail fashion (*58*).

It is clear from the above description of the *peplos* and the *chiton* that both these beautiful and elaborate garments were made of uncut lengths of material draped and fastened round the body. The only sewing was in the joining of the selvedges. What appear to be sleeves in the feminine *chiton* of the late archaic period are really formed by the fastenings. Tight-fitting sleeves are a foreign element in Greek costume (*55*).

In the classical period from 480 to 325 B.C. the masculine costume was the *chiton*, either short, or shortened by belting (*66, 68*). The long, pleated *chiton* of linen (*69*) was, however, worn to denote certain occupations and functions, e.g. by drivers at races, musicians and actors. The man's cloak was still the large, loosely draped *himation* (*69*), but the Thessalian cloak, or *chlamys*, fastened with a brooch on the right shoulder and leaving the right arm free, was also worn either alone (*71*) or over a short *chiton* (*65*). The vase paintings show that a stiff, square, patterned cloak, perhaps of felt, was sometimes worn by horsemen (*60*).

With the beginning of the classical period after the Persian Wars came a change in women's costume. The old-fashioned woollen *peplos*, discarded during the late archaic period, was given a new lease of life. It was now called the 'Doric' *peplos* as against the 'Ionic' linen *chiton*, which was still worn although it contained less material than before (*64*). The Doric *peplos* of classical Greece was regarded as a return to the simpler costume of ancient times, but it was not the same garment as the *peplos* of the archaic period (cf. *62* and *44*). The classical

peplos was full and fell in graceful folds, in contrast to the close-fitting archaic *peplos;* its material had a woven border but no pattern, whereas the other was patterned; and it was not sewn together in a tubular shape but the right side was left open (*62, 63, 70*). It could be worn loosely draped without a belt (*70*)—a style which gave the Spartan women the nickname of 'the hip-showing ones' (*63*)—or with a belt. If a belt was worn it was placed lower down and tied over the overfold, which had increased in length (*62*).

Both the classical Doric *peplos* and the *chiton* worn during the same period were clearly designed to resemble a column, the characteristic shape of the Greek feminine costume. The curves of the female figure were concealed by the fullness of the material and its rich folds. A belt usually held the dress in position, but that was its only function, for it did not emphasize the slenderness of the waist. The dress gave the body a unity, and every inclination and gesture was accompanied by the movement of its folds.

Doric column   *Ionic column*

These two costumes exemplify the difference between the Doric and Ionic styles of architecture. The Doric column, with its wide flutings, had no base but rested firmly on the stylobate and was crowned by a circular cushion-like member, the *echinus*, and a square member, the *abacus*. Similarly, the classical *peplos* gave to the feminine form a somewhat heavy look, the long overfold falling as an unbroken surface over the thick folds of the woollen drapery. The Ionic conception of form is different. Light and slender, with narrower fluting, it rests on a base and bears an intricate volute-capital. The pleating of the Ionic linen *chiton* was far lighter than the heavy folds of the Doric *peplos*, and its large false sleeves gave a width to the upper part of the body which corresponded to the curving capital of the column.

In time the difference between the two garments gradually disappeared. The *chiton* lost its false sleeves and acquired the overfold of the *peplos*, while the material used for the *peplos* was more finely woven. The belt also moved upwards, giving the female figure the slimness of the early archaic period (*72, 73*).

With the Hellenistic period, introduced by the campaign of Alexander the Great in India, Greece was brought into contact with the East. Cotton and silk were imported and woven with flax into a semi-transparent, gauzy material called 'Coan', after the island of Cos. At the same time women began to adopt the oriental custom of embroidering their dresses with gold and silver thread.

Greek costume made full use of the effects which could be obtained from unseamed garments. It displayed the height and width of the human form, but concealed all detail. Every movement was emphasized by its constantly changing folds, and Greek dress was especially capable of expressing the difference between movement and repose. It was governed by the same lucidity and the same monumentality as characterized Greek art and architecture.

Italy

The Etruscans
c. 1000–300 B.C.
(Figs. 74–87)

The Etruscans inhabited that part of Italy which is now called Tuscany. They are believed to have left Asia Minor and emigrated to Etruria, which was rich in minerals, in about 1000 B.C. By about 550 B.C. they had occupied a region extending from the Alps in the north to Lucania in the south, where their neighbours were the Greek colonists of Southern Italy. In the fourth century B.C. Northern Italy was conquered by the Gauls and Rome was expanding from the south, but the Etruscans were the cultural leaders in Central Italy until about 300 B.C.

Etruscans dancing and playing the flute

The Etruscans have left behind them many brilliantly coloured, vigorous frescoes on the walls of their underground tombs at Corneto, Chiusi, Orvieto, Vulci and Veji. These tombs were built from about 700 to 300 B.C. and the decorations portray the odd mixture of banquets, gladiatorial combats, flute-playing and dancing which accompanied an Etruscan funeral. The figures provide a rich field for the study of Etruscan costume.

The male dress was either a long *chiton* (*76, 77*) resembling the Greek ceremonial *chiton*, or a short *chiton* shaped rather like a doublet (*78*). But more important than the *chiton* was the cloak. It could be worn transversely below the right arm and across the left shoulder (*77*), either alone or over the *chiton*, or wrapped round the lower part of the body like a long skirt (*81*), or draped over both arms like a stole (*82, 86*). It was related to the loosely draped *himation* of the Greeks, while at the same time, in the method of draping which eventually became traditional (*87*), it also foreshadowed the Roman *toga*.

The oldest feminine dress was of thick material (*74, 75*), but this later gave place to a loosely hanging, beltless *chiton* of transparent, spotted material (*79, 85*). Accompanying it was a large square cloak, worn symmetrically over both shoulders (*85*). The lining was often in a contrasting colour (*79*).

A characteristic feature of Etruscan costume is the footwear. Many of the figures in the tomb paintings, both men and women, wear closed shoes with heel-pieces at the back and pointed, turned-up toes (*74, 79*). These are similar to the pointed shoes worn by the Hittites in Asia Minor, and reappear in the Gothic costume of the Middle

Ages. Any exaggeration in the length of the foot is usually accompanied by a high head-dress. With the Etruscans this was a cap shaped like a beehive (*79*), with or without a veil. This later became part of the clerical robes of the Roman priesthood. Instead of caps, women often wore pearl diadems in their hair, and the men fillets (*81, 83*).

In the later tomb paintings funeral dances and games are replaced by incidents from Greek mythology. The patterned materials and the beehive caps disappear, and sandals (*83*) are worn instead of pointed shoes.

Rome

c. 700 B.C.–A.D. 476

(*Figs. 88–99*)

The traditional date for the foundation of Rome is about 700 B.C. By 300 B.C. the Romans were the leading power in Italy; in 146 B.C. they conquered Greece; and soon after they were firmly established in Asia Minor. Syria, Gaul and Egypt had been annexed by the middle of the first century B.C. The Roman Empire was thus created in the centuries immediately before the beginning of the Christian era. It was a republic until 27 B.C., when Octavian was proclaimed Emperor with the title of Augustus.

Roman feminine costume

Although conquered by the Romans, the Greeks exerted a powerful influence on Roman art and culture, and Roman costume was likewise based on Greek. The Greek *chiton* and *peplos* reappear in the Roman feminine costume as the *tunica* (*89, 91, 97*). This was a house dress, but worn over it was the *stola* (*90*), and over this again the cloak, or *palla* (*98*). The head could be covered either by the cloak or by a veil (*90*). Greek women never wore more than two garments, but the Roman costume consisted of several. Like Greek women of the later period, Roman women wore girdles tied below the breasts, thus giving slimness to the figure and length to the legs. The material used was either finely woven wool or a mixture of wool and silk, the silk being imported across Asia from the mysterious and remote Seres, who, according to Pliny, found 'fine threads' on the leaves of trees which they spun and then wove into cloth. It was not until later that the secret of the silkworm was discovered. Roman women thus wore Chinese silk in spite of the vast distance it had to travel, and as it was light in texture and yet durable, the finished article was the most valuable merchandise of the ancient world. Silk became so popular that it was profitable to send it by the 'Silk Road', as the route across Asia was called. The caravans with their precious cargo climbed over vertiginous mountain passes, skirted precipices and crossed the trackless deserts of Central Asia, following the Chinese wall as far out as possible before going to Lopnor, the desert town which owed its existence as a commercial centre to the course then taken by the river Tarim. From there they followed the road through the country which is now known as Turan.

Underneath her light *tunica* the Roman woman wore a scarf or band to support the breasts. On her feet were sandals. Her hair was arranged in an elaborate coiffure. Apart from statues and reliefs, representations of the Roman feminine costume are also found on wall-paintings in the villas excavated at Pompeii, which was a summer resort for wealthy Romans until it was destroyed by an eruption of Vesuvius in A.D. 79.

The male *tunica*, which was sleeveless, was worn as an indoor dress and was pulled up over the belt like a blouse. Only workmen and slaves appeared in the *tunica* alone. The Roman citizen wore a cloak over it, the Roman *toga*, which is the masterpiece of the draped garments of antiquity. Neither before nor since has such a magnificently imposing and complicated garment been created out of a simple plain piece of material without cutting or fastening with pins or buckles. Wool was the material used for the toga; it was usually white, but senators and knights wore it with a purple band along the border.

The characteristic draping of the toga can already be seen in the oldest toga known to us, that worn by the 'Arringatore', an Etruscan statue of about 300 B.C. found in Lake Trasimene (*92*). It was semicircular in shape, thus differing from the Greek cloak, which was always oblong. A row of parallel folds was arranged along the straight edge before the cloak was put on. It was then placed on the *left* shoulder, the folds up against the neck, the rest of the material falling straight down and covering the left arm. In front the point of the cloak reached the knees, while behind the material was passed round the back, *under the right arm*,

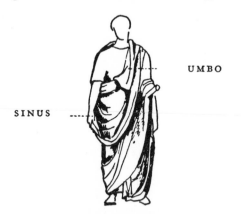

SINUS

UMBO

Imperial Roman toga

across the chest, and once more over the *left* shoulder, from where the second loose end hung down at the back. As the drapery went over the left shoulder a second time, another layer of folds was placed next to the first one.

The layer of folds was the motif which was developed further as the toga increased in size. During the Empire it evolved into a superbly decora-

tive garment with folds draped round the body like a cape and covering it completely.

The great toga of Imperial Rome evolved from the semicircular to an elliptical shape 4–5 yards long and about 3 yards wide, and was made of finely

Toga seen from behind

woven wool. Before being put on, it was folded lengthwise and thus became semicircular, like the toga of the 'Arringatore'.

It was also draped in exactly the same way. The top layer of material resting on the right hip, called the *sinus*, sometimes went over the head (*94*). The end of the cloak hanging down from the left shoulder next to the body was so long that to prevent it from trailing on the ground it was pulled outwards so that the folds hung in a pocket (*umbo*) over the rest of the toga and level with the left side of the chest.

Very occasionally the toga was draped over the right shoulder instead of below the right arm, so that both shoulders were covered and the right arm could rest in the loop formed by the folds (*93*).

Eventually the toga reached its maximum size. All the effects of which it was capable had been exploited, and it was no longer possible to carry a greater weight of material draped round the body.

It then began to lose its amplitude, and at the same time it was fixed in position, although not with pins or brooches. Throughout its long history, the toga never became a *fastened* cloak but was always kept in place by its own folds.

As explained above, the oldest toga (*92*) went twice over the left shoulder and two layers of folds were placed next to one another. The large elliptical toga, folded double, was arranged in the same way. During the late Empire it was secured by pulling the layer of folds nearest the neck over the second layer and drawing it tight over the shoulder in a wide, decorative band of parallel folds (95).

In its most elaborate form the toga of the early Empire completely covered the *tunica* worn as an undergarment, but as it grew smaller the *tunica* became more visible and therefore more important.

Originally the *tunica* had been sleeveless but so wide across the shoulders that the upper arm was partly covered (92, 94). A belt round the hips prevented it from appearing under the hem of the toga.

During the late Empire men began to wear the *tunica* with long sleeves. St Augustine, writing in the fifth century of this change in fashion, remarks: 'The old Romans considered it disgraceful to wear ankle-length tunics with sleeves, but now the upper classes consider it disgraceful not to do so.'

It became the practice to wear several sleeved tunics one over the other (95). They were of different cut, one with long narrow sleeves, another with wide open sleeves. When spread out, the latter resembled the letter T, and in the Emperor Diocletian's Maximal Tariff, a decree fixing the price of clothing, it is called a *dalmatica*. Originally

from the East, it was a loose garment trimmed with two long stripes called *clavi*, which began by being purple and later became red. It was introduced during the second century A.D. and, as we shall see, had a long life.

The toga finally ended its long history as a wide band draped round the body in more or less the same way as the toga had been, stiff with embroidery and richly adorned with precious stones. We find this band as part of the consular costume in the sixth century, and it was also preserved in the imperial robes of Byzantium (121, 123, 124).

But the toga was not the only cloak worn by the Romans. There was also the loosely draped *pallium* (96), actually the oblong Greek *himation* (cf. 45), which under its Roman name became the usual garb of philosophers and others who had neither the time nor the inclination to adjust and wear the complicated Roman toga.

The *pallium* later became the cloak worn by Christ, the Apostles and the many saints of the Roman Catholic and Greek Orthodox churches in the religious art of the Byzantine period and the Middle Ages. It was taken over by the Protestant countries after the Reformation and can still be seen in religious paintings and sculpture of the present day.

Byzantium

c. 300–1450

(Figs. 100–139)

Byzantium, later called Constantinople and today Istanbul, became the second capital of the Roman Empire shortly after the accession of Constantine the Great in 324. In 395 the Roman Empire was divided into two parts, one in the west with its capital in Rome, the other in the east with its capital in Byzantium. The Western Empire soon began to decline. Ever since the reign of Marcus Aurelius the Goths and Teutons had been raiding the northern provinces of Italy, which they eventually occupied, and in 476 the leader of the Teutonic armies, Odoacer, dethroned the last Roman Emperor. The Eastern Empire, in which Constantine the Great had made Christianity the official religion, held out for over a thous-

and years until in 1453 it was overrun by the Turks.

The various elements which combined to form Byzantine culture can be clearly discerned in Byzantine costume. The situation of Byzantium at the entrance to the Black Sea made Asia a close neighbour, and although the traditions of Roman dress were continued, they were strongly influenced by the Orient. It was, too, a region in which the traditions of the Greek costume of antiquity had not entirely disappeared.

Byzantine costume falls into three categories: the costume always worn by Christ and the Saints in the church mosaics, here called the dress of sacred figures; the ceremonial or ecclesiastical robes of bishops and priests; and the secular dress worn at the Byzantine court.

The dress of sacred figures was the *dalmatica* and cloak, the *dalmatica* being a sleeved *tunica* brought to Rome in the third century from the province of Dalmatia, which then included modern Dalmatia, Croatia and parts of Bosnia and Herzegovina. Even today the most important garment in the national dress of the women of this region is a long tunic of exactly the same cut as the ecclesiastical *dalmatica*.

In the dress of sacred figures the *dalmatica* was a wide garment with many folds worn without a belt; it had a horizontal neck-opening and was ornamented with two vertical stripes, the *clavi* (*100*). The cloak, which was the Roman *pallium* derived from the Greek *himation*, was loosely draped round the body in ample folds which did not fall into any definite pattern. It could cover the whole body (*101, 128*), or rest on the left shoulder (*103, 105, 115, 127, 129*), or over both shoulders (*104*), or it could cover the shoulders and arms (*116*).

The dress of the female sacred figures is the costume of the Roman matron with the addition of a veil (*102, 118*). They also wear a veil when they are shown in the ordinary feminine costume of the period (*114*).

The dress of sacred figures preserved not only the cut of the garments of Greece and Rome but, more important, their characteristics, i.e. loosely draped folds, plastic effects and capacity for emphasizing every movement. The Greek and Roman stylistic concepts were thus preserved.

The second category comprises the ecclesiastical robes worn by bishops and priests and includes the *dalmatica* and the chasuble (*109*). The chasuble was originally a Roman travelling cloak with a hood, but the hood gradualy shrank to a shield-shaped embroidered panel onl the back. The name of the large Roman cloak, the *pallium* (*109, 138, 139*), was erroneously transferred to a long woollen band embroidered with crosses. At first these ecclesiastical robes retained the many folds of the Greco-Roman costume, but in time they gradually grew stiff with embroidery and enveloped the body like a costly casket from which only the arms and head protruded.

The third category of Byzantine dress is the secular costume worn by men and women at court and later adapted and developed in Russia (*123,*

124). It can be seen in the Ravenna mosaics of the Emperor Justinian and the Empress Theodora with their retinue (*106–113*). It breaks away from the traditions of Greece and Rome, and the Oriental influence which was such an essential part of Byzantine culture is now in the ascendant.

The masculine costume (*107, 108*) consists of a girt-up *tunica* with long sleeves and a large cloak fastened with a buckle on the right shoulder. In general, the Byzantine masculine costume concealed much more of the body and limbs than the Greco-Roman costume. The long sleeves, which we still wear, now appear, and closed shoes replace sandals. The cloak falls over the left arm and hand and covers the greater part of the body. There are, it is true, folds in the drapery, but they are no longer the dominant feature. A large rectangular panel of embroidery, the *tablion*, appears both on the front and back of the cloak.

The Emperor Justinian wears a crown adorned with precious stones (*108*), but he is outshone by the magnificent jewellery of his consort (*111*). An elaborate diadem glitters on her brow, jewelled chains hang at either side of her head, and round her neck is a wide jewelled collar reminiscent of the Egyptian shoulder-cape.

The Empress's tunic, which reaches down to her pearl-studded shoes and is decorated with a wide band of gold embroidery at the hem, is almost concealed by a voluminous purple cloak. This, like the Emperor's, is fastened with a brooch at the right shoulder, but instead of the rectangular *tablion*, a frieze of figures is embroidered in gold along the lower edge.

The ladies of the Empress's court (*112, 113*) wear tunics woven of gold thread with embroidered or woven designs. The shawls round their necks and shoulders have that appearance of being at the same time soft and heavy which is characteristic of materials woven of gold or silver thread.

In the women's costumes we see even more clearly than in the men's that all Asia's treasures of cloth of gold and silver, of pearls and precious stones, were utilized for Byzantine dress. The woven material was of silk. This was at first imported (as in Rome) either as thread or as finished cloth, but in about 550 two monks, said to have been Persians, succeeded in bringing the larvae of the silkworm moth to Byzantium hidden in their hollow pilgrim's staffs, and so the manufacture of silk in Europe began.

What made Byzantine costume distinctive was not, however, the silk itself but the mixture of silk and gold thread. The use of material woven with gold thread and adorned with pearls and precious stones makes it quite different from the costume of Greece and Rome. Light does not play over the folds of a plain material as in the Greco-Roman costume; on the contrary, the light is caught and reflected as in one of the glowing mosaics on the walls of the churches. Byzantine costume is a complex of glittering details rather than a unity. An irresistible splendour takes the place of plastic effects.

The Middle Ages

Romanesque Period

c. 800–1200

(Figs. 140–165)

About a hundred and fifty years ago people began to develop a historical sense, and just as Vitruvius, the Roman architect who lived in the reign of Augustus, had classified the orders of Greek architecture as Doric and Ionic, so the early nineteenth century coined the word 'Romanesque' for the architecture of the early Middle Ages, thus indicating its derivation from Rome in the same way as the Romance languages are derived from Latin. The term is, however, somewhat misleading, since the Germanic peoples contributed as much, if not more, to the formation of this style.

The main feature of the Romanesque style is the rounded arch, which the Romans found in Asia Minor and adapted to their own use. The Romanesque building is usually a squat structure with thick walls and small windows. In the paintings of the period the human figure is portrayed in a rigid pose with the lines of the dress artificially twisted. All Romanesque art shows certain primitive characteristics.

The Romanesque style flourished from about 800 to 1200. Valuable information about the costume of the period can be obtained from contemporary illuminated manuscripts, which were executed with wonderful patience and care.

One fundamental difference between the Romanesque and the Byzantine costume is immediately obvious. It was noted in 968 by Bishop Liutprand on his return from an ambassadorial mission to Constantinople: 'The ruler of Greece wears long hair, trailing garments, wide sleeves, and a feminine head-dress. He is a liar and a swindler. The King of the Franks, on the other hand, wears beautiful short-cut hair, *a dress which is quite different from that of a woman*, and a cap.' He thus defines the distinction between Romanesque and Byzantine costume: in the former, men and women were differently dressed.

A new garment now makes its appearance in the masculine costume: trousers or leggings.

During the Greco-Roman period trousers were not part of the dress of the civilized peoples of the Mediterranean. The barbarians had worn them long before the beginning of the Christian era, and in Herodotus's time, c. 400 B.C., they were worn by the Medes and Persians. Herodotus tells us that a Lydian warned King Croesus: 'Sire, you are preparing to give battle to men who wear trousers of leather.' On the Greek vases the Amazons are depicted in this Asiatic trouser suit (55); and Cicero uses the expression *braccatae nationes* (trousered nations) as a general description of the barbarian peoples.

Trousers were introduced to the Romans by the Gauls and first appeared in Rome as short knee-breeches. One can understand the sensation which this strange foreign garment must have made, since the country of its origin was named after it—*Gallia braccata*. They were worn by the Roman soldiers stationed in the colder provinces in the north, and gradually made their way to Rome. The first tailors, who appeared in the city during the reign of Diocletian (A.D. 284–305), were called 'trouser makers'.

These short Gallic knee-breeches were not, however, the only kind of trousers: there were also the long Oriental trousers of the Persians,

Germans in long trousers

which spread northwards to the Dacians, the Marcomanni and the Scythians, and thence made their way to the German tribes. On Trajan's column, erected in A.D. 113, the Germans are shown with these long trousers.

The short Gallic knee-breeches now disappeared from history, but the long leggings introduced by the Germans became part of the Romanesque male costume. Besides leggings, this consisted of a tunic and cloak, the tunic knee length and with long sleeves (*147, 148, 154*). It was a wide, loose, closed garment worn with a belt. The cloak was fastened by a brooch on the right shoulder (*144, 145, 150, 151*), like the Greek *chlamys*.

Einhard, a contemporary of Charlemagne, describes this costume as follows: 'He (Charlemagne) was dressed in the manner of his fathers. Next to his body he wore a linen shirt, and linen drawers. Over these was a dress trimmed with silk, and leggings. Bands were wound round his legs, and his feet were clothed in shoes. He wore a dark blue cloak.'

There was another 'tunic' which went with the Romanesque male costume, namely, the mail shirt. In the Bayeux tapestry it is worn with a helmet fitted with a nose-guard (*152*), and is shown not only as it was worn by warriors but also alone, so that one can study its shape. It is in the form of a cross (cf. the *dalmatica*) but the skirt is slit down the middle at the front and back to allow freedom of movement. These slits are also carefully depicted in the Bayeux tapestry when the mail shirt is worn, with the result that it has often

been erroneously described as a garment ending in short trousers (*152*).

The long Byzantine tunic and the large cloak still formed part of men's attire in the Romanesque period. Charlemagne wore a long tunic during his visit to Rome, although reluctantly, since normally he always wore the short Frankish costume. But in 876 we hear that his grandson Charles the Bald appeared in a long robe on special occasions after his return from Italy, and in about 1000 Otto III is depicted wearing the long, Byzantine costume as his coronation dress (*143*).

The early mediaeval interpretations of the clothing of biblical and sacred figures was still Byzantine in character, and the traditional costume of *dalmatica* and cloak continued to be worn by Christ, the Virgin and the Saints (*141, 142, 155*). There is, however, a gradual change in the colours used. The Romanesque period liked colour and, in contrast to the purple of Byzantium glittering with gold and precious stones, it employed pure, vivid tones such as sky-blue, leaf-green and scarlet. The choice of colour soon became of great importance in paintings showing the dress of sacred figures (*146*).

Types of Romanesque costume

Women's costume consisted of two woollen tunics, a cloak and a kerchief. The head covering, first introduced in the dress of the Roman woman (cf. *90*), persisted in the Romanesque period, and another garment, the chemise of linen or silk, was added to the feminine wardrobe. The cloak was fastened with a brooch at the breast (*149*). The early mediaeval love of bright, pure colours is also shown in women's dress, which differs in this from Byzantine costume in spite of a similarity in cut.

One garment deserves special mention because of its importance later: the hooded cloak. Already known in Rome as a travelling cloak and as the dress of slaves, it became a church vestment, the chasuble (cf. *109*). In the Romanesque period the closed hooded cloak was used by clerics (*157*), by shepherds (*162, 163*) and by pilgrims (*159*). Towards the end of the period the hood tended to grow larger when worn by laymen, and developed a bag-like appendage at the back (*166*).

To summarize: in the Romanesque costume of western and northern Europe *c.* 800–1200, the dress of the sacred figures was derived directly from the costume of Byzantium. The introduction of trousers in non-ecclesiastical dress differentiated between men and women, and, apart from an interruption in the early Gothic period, continued to do so up to the present. Both men's and women's costumes followed the natural lines of the body, that is, neither its height nor its breadth was exaggerated. They combined elements which can be traced back to Roman costume with others showing the influence of peoples who in classical times lived outside the frontiers of the Roman Empire.

Gothic Period

c. 1200–1480

(*Figs. 167–232*)

During the Renaissance, when enthusiasm for the Greece and Rome of antiquity had reached its peak, Vasari (1511–1574), a painter and leading art critic of his day, said of the architecture of the immediately preceding period that it had been invented by the Goths who had destroyed the ancient buildings and filled Italy with monstrosities so hideous that other countries should pray God to save them from a similar fate.

Vasari's ironical term 'Gothic' is still used today, though we now realize that the Gothic style, which originated in France, had no connection with the Goths of the period of the great migrations. But, like 'Baroque', it is no longer used disparagingly. The Gothic period is one to which people have since turned for inspiration in art and literature, especially in nineteenth-century England.

As in Romanesque art, the key to the period style is the arch. The Gothic arch was, however, no longer semi-circular but pointed, and constantly increased in height until it eventually subsided to a flattened ogival form.

The Crusaders saw the pointed arch in Mohammedan architecture and brought the idea back with them. Its use led to buildings quite different from those based on the round arch. With the Gothic arch and rib-vaulting rooms could be made

surprisingly high and narrow. Horizontal lines seem to disappear; one is aware only of vertical lines. At the same time the framework is visible to the eye, not only in the lofty cathedrals which the citizens of the newly built towns laboured for generations to complete, but in the skeleton of the mediaeval half-timbered house with its black tarred beams embedded in the walls.

Gothic window

The Gothic, which succeeded the Romanesque in about 1200 and lasted in northern Europe until about 1500, is entirely opposed to the classical conception of style. We find in it none of the self-sufficient harmony of the Greek temple. Fanciful, eccentric and reaching airily towards the sky, it seems to ignore the limitations imposed by its material and even makes light of the law of gravity.

The figures in the wonderfully execu.ed miniatures which embellish the illuminated manuscripts of the period wear contemporary dress, as did those of the previous period. We learn from them that both the masculine and feminine Gothic costume broke clean away from all the ancient traditions.

Romanesque costume, like Byzantine costume, accepted the natural human stature and did not exceed the crown of the head or the sole of the foot. Gothic costume went beyond these limits, and in addition gave slenderness to the body and emphasized the vertical line, like the architecture which was contemporary with it.

The long Byzantine tunic, worn only on special occasions and by royalty (143, 153), now became the usual dress for men. Discovered by the Crusaders when they passed through Byzantium on their way to the Holy Land, it was brought back to Europe along with the pointed arch, but was not at first accepted with any great enthusiasm.

When it was eventually adopted, the long tunic entered on a period of development as the most important garment in the masculine wardrobe. Until then the cloak had been the mark of the free man and was only taken off as a sign of respect. This is evident from the advice given by a king to his son in a thirteenth-century Scandinavian manuscript called *The King's Mirror*. In one passage he says: 'You should enter the presence of the king without a cloak.' Elsewhere he mentions that whenever men of breeding appear before their liege lord they should not wear their cloaks, and that whoever is ignorant of this rule shows he is a churl.

During the early Gothic period, however, the main garment was the tunic, which was duplicated. Men now wore two long tunics, the outer (called the *surcoat*) being sleeveless (177, 179). But the lack of adequate heating made it impossible to discard the cloak (179) entirely and, lined with fur, it continued to be worn both at home and on journeys (182, 189). The surcoat was also given a fur lining (184), as were the short capes of the period (194); in fact, in the dress of the Middle

Ages fur was both utilitarian and decorative.

As a military garment the surcoat was worn over chainmail (167, 168, 175, 176).

The Gothic predilection for slender, elongated forms was shown in these long, loose tunics, which were exactly the same for both sexes, so that it is sometimes difficult to decide whether they belong to a man or a woman (184, 185).

With the long tunic went pointed shoes. Later they were developed further, but even during this period they extended beyond the natural length of the foot (182, 184, 188, 189, 191, 193) and initiated an exaggerated fashion which corresponded perfectly to the age's liking for elongated forms. The

Pointed shoes

pointed shoes had thin soles and were without heels. Heels did not make their appearance until much later.

Not only did the long tunic make the cloak unnecessary—a development corresponding to the shrinking of the Roman toga and its replacement by the *tunica*—but since it reached right down to the feet, it also led to the disappearance of leggings. These were now divided into two sections, the upper becoming underwear, usually of linen and invisible, while the lower became hose of cloth or leather shaped like long stockings and fastened to a belt round the waist.

Part of men's attire at this time was the hood. In the early Gothic period the hooded cloak became so short that it was more hood than cloak.

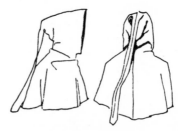

Hood with liripipe

The latter was reduced to a shoulder cape attached to the hood, while the point at the back of the hood (cf. *166*) was lengthened into a long, flat band, the liripipe.

This hood is especially characteristic of the masculine costume of the fourteenth century. It was worn by Dante and Petrarch, and appears in many contemporary portraits. Some original hoods of the period, from the graveyard at Herjolfsnaes in Greenland, are preserved in the National Museum in Copenhagen.

Hats, too, grew taller, with sugar-loaf crowns. The brim was turned up at the back and in front projected in a peak over the forehead (*191, 193, 194*). The Lateran Council of 1215 compelled Jews to identify themselves by wearing a round hat surmounted by a long, erect point (*178, 189*).

During this period the woman's cloak (*174*), like the man's, gradually lost its importance, although it too was retained as a rich, fur-lined garment against the cold (*183*). The woman's costume again resembled the man's in consisting of an undertunic with long tight sleeves and a sleeveless surcoat (*185*).

Another change in the feminine costume was as characteristic of the Gothic period as pointed shoes and hoods. When men's dress grew longer, thus overtaking, as it were, women's dress, the latter grew longer still, forming a train which trailed on the ground (*174, 181, 200, 201*).

Since both the tunics worn by women had this extra length, the surcoat was girt up to show the undertunic (*185, 186, 196*), and it was naturally desirable to choose the colours for the two tunics so that they harmonized.

Both men and women increased the effect of slenderness which these long costumes gave them by the peculiar posture fashionable at the time. The body took on the shape of an 'S', with the head inclined, the upper part of the body held well back, and the abdomen or one of the hips pushed forward (*184, 185, 186, 196*).

Both men and women wore their hair in long, loose curls often adorned with garlands of flowers (*184, 185*). As the men were beardless, their flowlocks combined with their long tunics often gave them a youthful and slightly feminine appearance.

Instead of a garland a young woman might wear a virgin crown (*181*), while a married woman covered her hair with a kerchief, either loose or tied under the chin and forming a coif (*174*).

In the early Gothic period the colours of the costume were of great importance. As has been mentioned, a woman showed her dress sense by choosing the colours of her undertunic and surcoat so that they harmonized. This led to something quite new, and to our minds very odd. Instead of wearing two differently coloured garments, two different colours were worn in the same garment on either side of a vertical dividing line down the body. This peculiar mediaeval fashion for wearing parti-coloured garments appears in both men's (*193*) and women's (*200*) clothing.

It persisted all through the Middle Ages, and beyond, in an even more exaggerated form, so that not only were tunics parti-coloured but hose as well (*206, 208, 212, 215*).

It was also fashionable to have a coat-of-arms embroidered on the costume. The knight wore his on the surcoat (*187, 197*) and on the trapper of his horse (*199*). With the rise of a hereditary nobility in the Middle Ages a knowledge of heraldry assumed great importance. Heraldic devices appeared not only on men's costumes but women too began to wear them on their surcoats (*200, 201*).

As well as a tendency to lengthen vertical lines, for example in the hood, pointed shoes and the train, the Gothic style emphasized structure. In dress this took the form of revealing the shape of the body, and was first apparent in women's costume. The armhole of the sleeveless surcoat was enlarged, and the undertunic made so tight that it clung to the body—a most ingenious way of emphasizing the feminine figure. It was, as it were, framed by the armholes, which were often trimmed with fur. They began by being quite small (*200*)

Woman's costume with 'Windows of Hell'

but were gradually extended until there was nothing left of the upper part of the surcoat but a narrow strip at the back and front. These large armholes reached their maximum size in about 1370 but can still be seen in pictures of a much later date (cf. *285*). An indication that they did not pass unnoticed but were, on the contrary, an over-whelming success is conveyed in their name, *fenêtres d'enfer* or 'windows of hell', which suggests the ascetic attitude of the Middle Ages to the temptations of the female body.

In masculine dress the Gothic emphasis on structure showed itself in a short, tight costume revealing the lines of the body which replaced the loose tunic in about 1350, a development related to the replacement of chain-mail by plate armour about the same time. Men as it were jumped out of their flowing draperies into a close-fitting costume consisting of a short doublet, long hose sewn together at the fork, and a codpiece (*221*).

Unlike the Romanesque short tunic or the early Gothic long robe, the tight doublet could not be pulled over the head, but was opened down the front and buttoned. It looks as if its wearers almost immediately regretted showing so much of themselves, for the doublet soon grew longer (*212, 213*) or the short costume was concealed under a voluminous gown with trailing sleeves, the *houppelande* (*209, 214*).

In the middle of the fifteenth century a most extraordinary decorative device appeared both on the gown and on other garments, an offshoot perhaps (as were the bells sewn on clothing) of that new and surprising development of the Gothic called 'flamboyant'. The edges of gar-ments were dagged into rows of fluttering oak leaves (*206–209, 214, 215*).

Gothic costume reached its culmination in a version worn chiefly in France and Burgundy. In the fourteenth and fifteenth centuries the Flemish towns of Bruges and Ghent were great centres of European trade and industry. Flemish cloth was famous everywhere, and the court of Burgundy shared the leadership of fashion with Paris. Simultaneously with the dawn of the Renaissance in Italy, Gothic costume here attained its final phase of richness and splendour.

The Burgundian costume is the apotheosis of the costume of the Middle Ages. All the sartorial variations which had gradually appeared during the period were somehow combined into a final magnificent flourish.

It included pointed shoes (*223, 224, 228*), tight fitting doublets, and large padded sleeves (*mahoîtres*) which increased the height of the shoulders and minimized the waist (*223*). The train of the feminine costume was more voluminous than ever before (*225, 226*) and at the same time the upper part of the dress was given a deep pointed opening at the front and the back and gathered under the breasts by a wide belt (*225, 226, 230*).

The Burgundian costume was richly trimmed with fur, which could be either miniver in men's capes (*229*) or an edging of ermine on the women's dresses. Women wore fur at the neck-line or covering the hands as wide cuffs to the narrow sleeves, or as a broad edge along the hem of the surcoat (*225*).

The long masculine gown was now worn with a large flat hat from which a wide strip of material or a ribbon, called the liripipe, hung over the shoulder (*231*).

The Burgundian costume also displayed the typical Gothic exaggeration of height. Men wore the high Burgundian cap (*224, 228*), while over the heads of the women rose the most peculiar of all the head-dresses created by the Gothic style— the *hennin*. This was a conical or steeple-shaped structure of metal, brocade or velvet. It first appeared in about 1375 and remained fashionable until about 1480. As it resembled the conical metal *tantura* worn by the women of Syria, the Crusaders may possibly have brought it home with them from Asia Minor, as happened with so many other ideas they came across during their travels.

Women shaved their brows and temples and

Man's costume with bells

completely concealed their hair under the pointed *hennin*. The shape of this conical frame corresponds amusingly with the inverted cone formed by the lower part of the costume. It was adorned either by a long, transparent veil which floated down behind (*226*), or by a tall construction of starched linen (*225, 230*). The *hennin* was the most sublime expression of the Gothic pre-occupation with elongated forms, although it was not the only kind of head-dress worn. The hair, too, could be arranged to make a woman look taller. A fillet-coiffure might rise from the head, or the hair above the shaven brow could be scraped upwards into two horns partly covered by veils (*211*).

The Renaissance

Italian Fashions

c. 1480–1510

(*Figs. 233–276*)

While the Gothic costume of the Middle Ages was reaching its final phase at the court of Burgundy, the first stirrings of the Renaissance brought a new conception of dress—or rather the revival of an old conception—in Italy. The Gothic style never really became acclimatized south of the Alps, where it had always been considered foreign and bizarre, its eccentricities quite alien to the sobriety of the classical style. Italy had, however, preserved the ancient traditions, and people now began to turn to them again. Early in the fifteenth century Florence became the centre of a revival of interest in the art of antiquity, especially that of the late Roman period. The new style which gradually emerged was a fresh exploration of Roman art and its ideals, not a direct imitation.

In the architecture of the Renaissance the horizontal line replaced the vertical line of the Gothic. Arches were round instead of pointed, and windows and doorways rectangular. Buildings, the most important of which were now palaces instead of cathedrals, were distinguished by firm, unbroken lines and symmetrical proportions. Towers and spires disappeared; the Renaissance church is crowned with a dome. The contemporary conception of style was defined in about 1480 by the architect Leon Battista Alberti, who said that perfection consists of a rational and harmonious concord of the parts, so that nothing can be added, subtracted or changed without impairing the general effect.

For generations the leading family in Florence had been the Medici. Lorenzo the Magnificent, who died in 1492, patronized Leonardo, Raphael and Perugino, and Botticelli was his court painter In the school for sculptors which he founded he met one day a remarkably gifted 14-year-old boy whose name was Michelangelo. But art also flourished in other Italian towns like Venice and Urbino, and the costumes of the period are faithfully reproduced in the works of contemporary painters.

The Italian Renaissance costume of the fifteenth century dominated European fashion until about 1510, when it was superseded by German-Swiss costume.

To appreciate the difference in line, colour and materials between the early Renaissance costume and that of the Gothic period it is necessary to study the development of Italian costume during the fifteenth century, so I propose to go back a little and describe some of the changes brought by the Renaissance to the version of the late Gothic costume which had reached Italy.

As has already been mentioned, the Gothic style never gained a firm foothold in Italy, and the characteristic features of Gothic costume appeared there in a weakened form. In about 1450 Italians wore either a short doublet with hose (*245, 246*), or an ankle-length gown concealing the body (*252*). The doublet could be buttoned (*247*), and the hose were either two long loose stockings of leather or cloth which could be unfastened from the belt and rolled down for work (*241, 247*), or they were wide at the top and sewn together to form one garment (*248*), with a cod-piece (*275*). This is the typical costume of the late Gothic period. But the shoes did not exaggerate the length of the foot, and the only trace of shoulder padding, the late Gothic *mvhoîtres*, was a widening of the sleeves at the shoulders (*245, 246, 253*). The large flat hat with the liripipe (*243*) of the late Gothic period was also worn as was the high-crowned hat resembling an inverted flower pot. (*251*, cf. *209*). But the trend seems to have been more towards turban head-dresses (*233, 239*).

A number of diluted Gothic elements also appeared in the woman's dress of the period, which consisted of an over- and under-gown and a cloak or coat with hanging sleeves. The Italian feminine costume had a train and a high belt (*249, 250*) like the contemporary Burgundian costume, but it did not have its deep V-shaped décolletage. There were garments with dagged edges (*250*), but the high head-dresses designed to conceal the hair and add height to the figure did not cross the Alps. Instead, flat head-dresses (kerchiefs) were worn or the hair was arranged round the head in plaits wound in some light transparent material. A faint trace of the odd Gothic fashion for shaving the front of the head and temples can be seen in the way Italian women combed their hair off the brow (*249, 250*).

From the middle of the fifteenth century various signs of Renaissance influence became apparent: patterned fabrics were used instead of materials in a single colour, and silk, velvet and brocade replaced wool. The Italian silk weavers produced magnificent fabrics woven with gold and silver (*238, 259, 262*). These materials remained pictorial rather than sculptural in their effects and were worn either spread out to show the patterns to their best advantage or arranged in regular parallel folds.

These sewn folds became a very important feature in the Italian masculine fashions of the early Renaissance. They can be seen in the sleeveless cloak worn by knights in armour (*233, 237*) and in the bell-shaped doublet which flares out below and is gathered in heavy folds at the waist (*245*).

Besides these new materials, another, hitherto carefully concealed, now made its appearance— the white linen of the shirt. In 1250 the father in *The King's Mirror* had already expressed the opinion current at the time when he earnestly advised his son always to have his shirt cut a good deal shorter than his tunic, since no well-bred man would admit to wearing hemp and flax.

But times had changed. In the masculine costume of the early Renaissance the shirt began to show. It reached halfway down the thigh, was slit at the sides (*247*), and had long sleeves but no collar. With laced outer sleeves it was visible along the underside of the arm (*248*), and could also be seen round the arm-hole since the sleeves themselves were now detachable and laced to the doublet with points (*270*). The shirt eventually appeared at the neck also, the man's doublet being cut low to display it, and its upper edge was embroidered in gold or silk (*264*).

With the fashion for low necklines, men's costumes became both shorter and wider, giving them a squarish appearance (*262, 263, 264*). The jerkin was lengthened and the gown shortened so that both reached halfway down the thigh, and the gown had a wide collar falling over the shoulders (*264*).

Very long gowns were now worn only by the elderly (*266*). Hat brims were turned up (*262*), or the hat reduced to a small skullcap fitting closely over the hair, which was shoulder length and either hung loosely or was curled under at the bottom (*263, 264, 268*).

Since the gown was now the same length as the jerkin, the doublet was reduced in size to a jacket, to which the hose, sewn together to form a single garment, were attached (*265*).

The peculiar Gothic fashion for parti-coloured dress was given a new lease of life in Italy (*261*).

The feminine costume of the early Renaissance was fully developed by the last quarter of the fifteenth century. Elderly women wore kerchiefs (*255, 257, 260*); young women did not cover their hair but adorned it with strings of pearls or a net (*256, 259, 274, 276*).

The lacing characteristic of the masculine dress also appeared in women's costumes, at the breast, under the arm, and at the shoulder, where the long tight sleeves were laced to the armhole (*258, 259, 267*).

Whereas elderly women still wore two long, loose, trailing gowns and a cloak, young women followed the masculine trend towards shorter gowns. The long gown of the women was caught up at the belt to form a sort of blouse, the extra length being bunched round the hips (*256*). This was a fashion which soon disappeared, but another innovation persisted: the gown began to lose its train (*259*). With this came the division of the gown into bodice and skirt. The two parts remained joined, but this was a development which foreshadowed the following period's emphasis on the 'platforms' of the body on which the clothes rested. The neckline became square (*274*), in contrast to the pointed Gothic neckline. The costume still consisted of an over- and an under-tunic, or, as they should now be called, a gown and an under-gown. Since women did not wish to conceal the under-gown, the material of which was just as beautiful as that of the gown itself, and

since it was inconvenient to raise the new stiff materials with a belt, the Italian fashion was to show the under-gown through a vertical slit in the front of the gown (*259*).

To summarize briefly, the characteristics of the Italian mode of the early Renaissance were: gorgeous patterned materials such as velvet, silk and gold and silver brocade; lacing at the breast, on the shoulders and under the arm; low necklines in the men's costumes, which became short and wide; and a tendency for women's robes to lose their train.

German Fashions

c. 1510–1550
(*Figs. 277–313*)

The evolution of the costume of the High Renaissance falls into two periods. During the first half of the sixteenth century German fashions were predominant, but from the middle of the century Spain took the lead.

The outstanding feature of the German mode was its original use of coloured fabrics. The parti-colouring of the Middle Ages and the patterned materials of the early Renaissance in Italy were also used in the German costume at the beginning of this period (*277, 278, 288, 291*), but were superseded by effects obtained by placing two fabrics of different colours one over the other. The outer garment was slashed to show the material underneath through the slits. In men's costumes the slashing of the hose and doublet began where they were tightest, i.e. on the legs and sleeves (*289, 298, 302*), and a rich lining in a contrasting colour was drawn out through the gaps. Later these slits, which were originally a Swiss fashion, were made all over the costume (*304*), even the shoes and cap being slashed and lined with material in various colours.

The slashing of the outer garment and the appearance of the lining through the slits created an interplay between two planes, one superimposed on the other. The effect was similar to that of the interpenetrating scrolls of the cartouche in contemporary ornament, in which tongues from one scroll pass through slits in another.

When it became too laborious for tailors to cut any more slits in the material, holes were burned into it with a red-hot iron. The lining which poured out through them was of thin, brilliantly coloured silk.

The function of costume in the Renaissance was to add width to the body, as is clearly shown in the masculine fashions. Here the important garment was the short gown, usually fur-lined and with hanging sleeves. It was loose, with ample folds, and a large collar covered the shoulders,

Cartouche work

making them appear wide and square (*308, 311, 313*).

The gown became the most important masculine garment, entirely replacing the cloak (*281, 286, 291*). In a lengthened form, it has been retained up to the present day as the cassock. The open front showed the jerkin, which had a gathered knee-length skirt (*311, 313*) and was sometimes cut very low in front to display the doublet (*311*). The early Renaissance fashion for a low neckline was much in vogue at the beginning of the period (*282*) but was later replaced by a costume which fitted closely round the neck. First the shirt, finely pleated, was cut high, to end as a standing collar (*313*), and the doublet gradually followed suit. When it also acquired a standing collar, the shirt was visible only as a small frill under the chin, the beginning of the ruff of the following period. Since the tendency was to exaggerate the width of the body, the fashion for long tight hose joined together at the top (*284, 298, 299, 302*) did not survive beyond the beginning of the period. Later the hose were partly covered by loose breeches from which the cod-piece, which grew increasingly prominent, emerged. The breeches were made of wide strips of material or panes joined together at intervals and with the lining drawn out through the gaps (*313*).

From these puffed breeches developed the extravagant *Pluderhose* of the German *Landsknecht*, or mercenary soldier, in which loose panes hung from hip to knee and unbelievable quantities of thin rustling silk cascaded out between them. Both the civil authorities and the clergy fulminated against them in vain, for from being the favourite garment of the *Landsknecht* they spread to all classes of society in the Protestant countries. In 1555 Bishop Musculus of Frankfurt published a fiery pamphlet against them: 'Any young lout must now, long before he has grown hair on his chin, spend more money on breeches and hose than his father needed for his wedding garments'; and in another passage he says: 'Our young fellows have their cod-pieces in front puffed out by the flames and rags of Hell so that the Devil can sit and look out in all directions, causing scandal and creating a bad example, nay, poor, giddy, innocent girls are seduced and enticed thereby.' The scandal was caused partly by the vast quantities of material used and partly by the extravagant dimensions of the cod-piece.

Landsknechte in Pluderhose

Shoes during this period became broad at the toes (*304, 311*), with slits which made them look even broader. The head-dress was a flat, wide-brimmed cap richly trimmed with ostrich feathers and placed on the head at an angle (*278, 283, 284, 288, 298, 308, 311, 313*). It was sometimes worn over another cap (*281, 289*). The long hair of the men of the early Renaissance was now cut short, and beards became popular (*290, 308, 311*).

The development of women's costume ran parallel with men's. At the beginning of the sixteenth century the kirtle had a square neckline (*305, 306*), the décolletage being covered by a small shoulder cape (*296*), but it gradually moved upwards and was worn with a standing collar. A small frill under the chin (*309*) resembled that of the masculine costume. Women's clothing at this time was usually voluminous and had the same exaggerated width as men's. The skirt was pleated, or pleated aprons were worn (*295, 296*). At the beginning of the period sleeves were wide, but they gradually became tight and were divided horizontally into sections round the upper arm (*301, 306, 307*), while later they were funnel-shaped (*312*). Head-dresses were flat (*277, 285, 292, 297*), and many of them have been retained in the nun's habit of today. One head-dress, however, was especially characteristic of the 'German style' of the Renaissance—the pearl cap which completely hid the hair. When a wide-brimmed cap trimmed with ostrich feathers was worn, it was set at an angle over the pearl cap (*305*).

The characteristic features of the German fashions were: slashing and puffing, costumes rising to the neck, the short wide gown of the masculine dress, hose and short puffed breeches developing into *Pluderhose*, broad-toed shoes, and the wide-brimmed cap worn by both sexes.

There is something both imposing and gay about the German fashions of the High Renaissance. Costumes were extravagant in their use of material and displayed a fondness for colour, but at the same time they were stately, comfortable, and elegant in a casual way.

Spanish Fashions

c. 1550–1600

(Figs. 314–335)

By about the middle of the sixteenth century Spain had assumed the lead in the world of fashion. The 'Spanish style' was strongly influenced by geometrical forms, the body being circumscribed by spheres, cones and circles which not only completely concealed its natural curves but emphasized the different 'platforms' such as the hips and shoulders.

The costume of the Spanish style was the greatest achievement of the art of tailoring, as the Roman toga was of the art of drapery. The Roman toga exploited to the full all the possibilities of the draped costume. Its living, moving folds played round the natural forms of the human body. In the Spanish costume the body was a stiff, motionless dummy on which was mounted a richly ornamented, skilfully wrought masterpiece of the tailor's art. The costume formed a case for the body, following its shape on the inside, but showing quite different contours on the outside. The wearer was adorned like an idol with gold, pearls and precious stones, all the riches which had poured into Spain with the discovery of America and the Indies. Since there were no safes or banks in those days, people carried their fortunes about on them, beaten into gold chains or encrusted on their clothes like an armour of precious stones. They did so partly because this was the safest place to keep them, partly to display their wealth. A similar outlook has persisted up to the present day in the Balkans, where girls carry their dowry sewn on to a coin-cloth hanging over the breast and in the old days the standing of a peasant was judged by the number and weight of the silver buttons on his jacket.

As a foil for this lavish display of jewellery, the Spanish fashions made use of black or dark-coloured silks and velvets, like the soft lining of a jewel case. This was the background on which the craftsmen in gold lace and pearl embroidery worked. Besides stitched-in jewellery and loose gold chains, there were also tags of gold or precious stones shaped like flowers which could be attached to the costume, where, like a swarm of golden beetles, they burrowed into the soft material wherever there was an empty space.

During the period when Spanish fashions were in the ascendant it is interesting to see how German costume adapted itself to the new ideas. At first we find the characteristic German wide-brimmed cap (315, 316, 318) and the early form of short, puffed breeches with panes (315, 316, 321).

The Spanish fashions replaced the wide-brimmed cap by a high-crowned hat with a narrow brim (319, 321), and the short gown by a circular short cloak with a collar—the 'Spanish cloak' —which was often richly lined with fur (316). The cod-piece was rarely seen after 1575, and finally disappeared when puffed breeches were ousted by short trunk hose stuffed with horsehair or some similar material to give them a distended shape (319, 330).

Simultaneously, stuffed shoulder wings were sewn round the arm-hole (319) and a short skirt was added to the doublet, which was padded in front. In contrast to the padding in the upper part of the body, the legs were enclosed in tight hose of cloth, velvet or linen. The first knitted stockings came from Spain and are mentioned as a present to Henry VIII in 1547. In 1589 William Lee invented the stocking frame, and from then on the seamed leg covering of the Middle Ages was replaced by the knitted stocking. Shoes became narrower and covered more of the foot and the knitted stockings, which were less hard-wearing than seamed hose. The stuffed breeches of the Spanish period were no longer gourd-shaped, but ended in a straight line at the bottom (334, 335).

The masculine costume was high-necked, the doublet with a standing collar and the shirt visible as a narrow frill under the chin (315, 316, 318, 319, 321). It was from this narrow frill that the most characteristic feature of the Spanish style developed: the circular ruff with hand ruffs to match (324, 327, 335). The collar grew larger and larger, and at its maximum size was called the 'millstone ruff'.

In the French and English versions of the Spanish fashions the stuffed doublet developed into what was called the 'peascod belly' (324, 327, 330, 332), formed by padding which produced a pointed bulge over the stomach. The short gourd-shaped breeches have survived until modern times in coronation robes (cf. 426).

The woman's costume followed the man's in the use of padding, the exaggeration of the width of the hips, and the emphasis on the horizontal line of the shoulders.

Two new garments made their appearance under the gown. One was the corset, at first of stiff material but later with steel stiffeners sewn into the lining. These, helped by padding, completely flattened the bust and hid its natural curves, so that the upper part of the feminine body was transformed by this *vasquine* or *basquine* into a cone with the point downwards.

Spanish farthingale

The other was the farthingale. Called the *vertugale* or *verdingale* in Spain, it was the first 'crinoline' in history. It was at first made of felt, but later hoops were employed to produce the shape of an upward-pointing cone over which the material was tightly stretched. The gown had a triangular

opening in front showing the underskirt (314, 317, 323). As in men's costumes, the circular ruff was tied under the chin (323, 325) and had cuffs to match. It later developed into the 'millstone ruff' (328).

The Spanish fashions in women's costume were considerably modified in France and England. Colours became brighter, and a padded roll was added to the conical farthingale which made the dress stand out round the hips (326). The cone was thus transformed into a drum (331). Its evolution can be clearly seen by comparing the illustration of Princess Elizabeth by 1547 (314) with the picture of her as Queen in the magnificent costume she wore

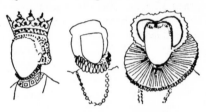

Development of the ruff

in 1592 (331). In the latter the ruff has as it were dropped from its position round the neck on to the top of the farthingale, over which its flounces are arranged like the lid on a hat box. The neckline has fallen again, and a starched lace collar rises behind. The starch for ruffs was originally light blue, but for a short period in about 1617 it was saffron yellow (333).

Towards the end of the 'Spanish period' the waists of both men's and women's costumes rose. Hitherto there had been a fashion for long pointed waists with the exaggerated width of the hips appearing below the natural hip line. The belt now moved up, taking with it the fullness of the hips, and the padding no longer produced angular or circular geometrical forms but a richly draped, well-rounded figure (328, 333).

These new designs were later to dominate the costume of the Baroque period.

Padded hip-roll under dress

With fashion, no precise date can be given for the end of one style and the beginning of another. The characteristics of one period can always be found in embryo in the preceding period, while traces of them linger on alongside features of the newer style which follows.

Baroque

c. 1620–1715
(*Figs. 336–393*)

If any one person can be said to have created a style, then Michelangelo, the great Italian painter and sculptor, was the father of the Baroque. For it was his predilection for vigorous movement and dramatic effects which formed the taste of a new generation of artists and architects in the period succeeding the Renaissance. The mediaeval masters had no name for the style in which they worked, and Michelangelo and his immediate successors did not use the word 'Baroque'. It was first employed in about 1800 to mean something extravagantly ornamental and bizarre, and therefore quite unlike the Empire style which was fashionable at the time.

The Baroque began in about the middle of the sixteenth century in Italy, continuing until about 1700 in Southern Europe and a little longer in Northern Europe. The clear, definite contours of the High Renaissance were succeeded by the

Auricular ornament

curved and broken lines of the Baroque. In architecture, the continuous straight line was avoided. Part of a building, such as the centre, the dome, or the portal, was brought into prominence at the expense of the rest. In painting, the figures were shown in violent motion. Ornament became mas-

sive and voluminous, with powerful contrasts of light and shade. Especially characteristic of the early Baroque period until the middle of the seventeenth century is the so-called 'auricular' ornament, which writhes, curls and twists like the cartilage of the ear, from which it derives its name. This predilection for vigorous movement is seen everywhere, and also in the costumes of the period.

In the early years of the seventeenth century none of the European courts was the undisputed leader of fashion. Holland, however, was in her heyday as a great commercial power, and the costume of the wealthy Flemish burghers was everywhere imitated. The Spanish fashions had divided the body into sections, with the emphasis on the hips and shoulders, but Dutch costume again made it a single unit and gave both men and women a full, rounded contour.

Women's dress was no longer stretched over a padded frame. Outside Spain both the corset and the farthingale disappeared, several skirts being worn instead to give the body the desired volume (*339*). The silhouette was barrel-shaped (*341, 343, 345, 352, 356, 359*), the waist line moved upwards, and below it both the dress and the figure became fuller, making women appear healthy, homely, and perpetually pregnant.

Fewer colours were used, black being the most common. Women still wore two gowns, one over the other. As a reminder of the drum-shaped Spanish or French farthingale, the overgown was for a time looped round the hips (*351*). The starched lace collar spread over the shoulders, giving them a rounded feminine slant (*341, 345, 352, 356*). The dress was often cut low, but the deep neckline was covered by yet another collar so that the dress was both low-cut and high-necked at the same time (*343*). The golden chains of the previous period were succeeded by strings of pearls in the hair, round the neck (*356*), over the breast, and sometimes round the waist as well. The sleeves, which ended in wide, turned-up lace cuffs (*343, 345*), were large and elegant, and were often gathered in at the elbow with silk ribbons finished in bows which divided them into two balloon-like sections (*341, 343, 345*). A similar silk ribbon sash with a bow emphasized the high waist-line (*341, 345*). Women's sleeves gradually became shorter, exposing part of the forearm (*356, 359*). During the early Italian Renaissance it was fashionable to be blonde, and women used every kind of preparation to turn their hair golden. The Flemish Baroque dress, however, required dark hair, and fair-haired women powdered it to make it brown. It was worn shoulder-length and uncovered, often with two long ringlets falling forward over the shoulders (*352*), the ends tipped with a bow or, still more charming, with a single white pearl.

The masculine costume also gradually assumed the high-waisted barrel-shaped silhouette (*337, 338, 344*), and the peascod belly disappeared. The skirt of the doublet was cut into loose overlapping tabs (*337, 338, 344, 349, 376*), and the waist-line was emphasized by a row of bows. These had originally been metal-tagged ribbons attached to the breeches and supporting them by being tied through eyelets in the doublet; later, when the breeches were fastened with straps to the inside of the doublet, the bows survived as ornaments (*344*).

Breeches lost their padding and after being baggy and loose (*337, 338*) became long and narrow and were fastened in front with exposed buttons (*362*). They now reached below the knees, where they joined a completely new kind of footwear, high-heeled leather boots with spurs, which replaced shoes (*344, 346, 347, 348, 353, 354, 355, 362*). Until 1630 they were similar in shape to the riding boots of today, but the tops were gradually widened and were pulled down, displaying the lace edging of the boot hose (*344, 348*) which were worn to protect the silk stockings. This was during the Thirty Years' War (1618–1648), and one would have thought that war and lace did not go well together. But far from it. Exquisitely worked and fragile as a cobweb, lace appears all over the military dress of the period; on the boot hose, the cuffs, the falling collar worn over both the doublet (*337, 344, 347, 348, 356*) and the cuirass (*346*), and

to trim the edge of the wide military scarves of taffeta tied round the waist (*346, 354, 355*).

The smooth white collar edged with scalloped lace had replaced the ruff, with its layers of tubular pleats which had gone so well with tightly stretched fabrics, but now that costumes were loose and full and brought out the contrast of light and shade, the collar became smooth and unpleated.

The change from ruff to lace collar developed differently in men's and women's costumes, and began first in the men's. In women's dress the high, starched, lace collar, like that in the picture of Queen Elizabeth (*331*), simply lost its starch and fell over the shoulders. In the masculine dress the development was more gradual. At first starch was not used, so that the ruff hung limply round the neck like a frill (*338, 349*). It was then replaced by a wide falling collar, or, in Spain where the use of lace was prohibited in 1623, by the *golilla*, a plain, round, under-collar which had been used to support the ruff but was now worn alone (*340, 342*). It eventually became a plain rectangular collar edged with lace and resembling that of the feminine costume (cf. *344* with *345*, *352* with *356*). The man's lace collar, which was tied under the chin with thin strings, was worn over the high collar of the doublet and spread out obliquely towards the shoulders. It is amusing to notice in the pictures of this period how elderly people stuck to the ruffs (*363*) which had caused such a scandal when they first appeared, while plain falling lace collars were worn by the young (*362*). After 1633 collars and cuffs of plain white linen, without lace, appeared in both the masculine and feminine costume (*358, 359*).

When the ruff disappeared men began to grow their hair longer (*346, 347*). It was often plaited on either side of the head in pigtails called *cadenettes* (*348*).

Men's hats were large, soft and broad-brimmed; usually of felt, they were decorated with flowing ostrich plumes and worn slightly tilted (*338, 349, 353, 354*). The same kind of hat could also be worn by women (*351, 352*). An important garment in men's attire was the short cloak which, unlike the Spanish cloak worn over both shoulders, was slung loosely across one shoulder (*348*) or draped theatrically round the body (*358*).

There is something very elegant and dashing about the male costume of 1630 to 1640. Its style and harmonious colours have been made familiar by the paintings of Van Dyck.

Towards the middle of the seventeenth century the Baroque style became even more sumptuous and dignified. The favourite ornament of the period was the acanthus of classical antiquity, now more exuberant and combined in decorative designs with nature's largest fruit and flowers; marble trophies were composed of cannons, weapons, Roman armour and helmets with flowing ostrich plumes. In architecture church façades were built with an eye to scenic effect, with undulating walls. In sculpture, draperies were shown in violent motion, and high-reliefs replaced bas-reliefs.

For the first time since the early Gothic period France again took the lead in art and costume. In 1643, at the age of five, Louis XIV ascended the throne which he was to occupy until his death seventy-two years later. During his reign everything connected with art and craftsmanship was organized, e.g. the Royal Academy of the Fine Arts was established, followed by the Academy of Architecture and a *manufacture de meubles*. Fashion and its dissemination was also organized from the Sun King's Court and from Paris, which, for the first time in history, can be called a fashion centre in the modern sense of the word. Previously various countries and cities had been the leaders of fashion, but without being conscious of it or attempting to turn it to their advantage. All this was now changed. In the latter half of the seventeenth century two full-sized dolls were sent from Paris across the Channel to London every month, and later to other European capitals as well. '*Les fameuses poupées*', as they were called, were in fact models for women's costumes. 'Big Pandora' was in *grande toilette*, 'Little Pandora' in the so-called *négligé*, i.e. travelling costume, house-coat or anything which was not *grande toilette*. Not even a war like the War of the Spanish Succession could hinder their journeys. It was also, of course, French workshops which produced the materials and the various accessories of fashion. Both the word 'mode' and the idea of being 'modern' date from this period.

In the latter half of the century women's dresses were cut low in a boat-shaped neckline and were worn either without a collar (*366–368*) or with a lace edging falling from the top of the bodice (*375*). Sleeves were three-quarters length and full, and **were** attached to the bodice below the sloping

A dandy c. 1670

shoulders (*366–368, 375*). The waist-line was natural. The bodice began to extend into a point overlapping the skirt, and corsets were re-introduced as a support (*375*).

The most interesting and remarkable developments during the period which coincided with the youth of Louis XIV were, however, in men's dress. The elegant, soldierly costume somehow disintegrated. Garments shrank until they no longer seemed to belong to one another, while the emphasis shifted to the shirt and the lavish use of bunches of silk ribbons. Simultaneously, leather boots were replaced by shoes with bows and long square toes.

The doublet became so short that it reached only just below the chest, and was worn open. The sleeves reached only to the elbow (*374, 377, 378*), so that the wide shirt sleeves, edged with lace and tied round with silk ribbon in several places (*374*), were visible. Boot hose disappeared, but their lace tops survived as wide ruffles below the knees (*369, 374, 376*). The breeches, decorated at the top with bunches of ribbon loops, hung low on the hips and revealed the shirt at the waist (*365*). They also changed their shape, becoming open and very wide in the legs so that they resembled a short skirt (*365, 369*). Called Rhinegrave breeches after the Rhinegrave of Salm who launched them in Paris, and petticoat breeches in England (*365, 369, 374, 376, 377, 378*), they were worn from about 1650 to 1680. The excessive trimming with silk ribbon loops, or *galants* as they were called— a Saxon police regulation of 1661 records that about 140 yards of silk ribbon were commonly used in a man's costume—produced an over-dressed and fussy appearance, and the costume seems to lose all definite outline. The shirt was now so much in evidence that it became an important garment. It was so conspicuous, with its rich lace trimming and elaborate decoration, that one would think it would have been kept clean, but the age had peculiar ideas about cleanliness. It was not fashionable to wash either oneself or one's linen too often, and perfume was used instead, the stronger the better. As linen was changed only once a month it was not necessary to have much of it, but what one did possess could be lavishly trimmed with lace. The round cloak worn over the shoulders (374) made a futile attempt to hide the curious disjointedness of the costume.

The whirling movement of the Baroque style had only a relatively short life. Both the style and the costume soon became quieter and more dignified.

The cloak was now discarded for the *casaque* (374), a long jacket or coat. Originating in the soldier's uniform, it was at first loose, but was gradually shaped to the figure, the skirt being gathered into wide, vertical pleats on the hips. The loose-fitting *casaque* (379, 380) then became the elegant, shaped *justaucorps* (381), which in fact fitted '*juste au corps*', closely to the figure. It was knee-length with large turned-back cuffs. Underneath, the skirt-like Rhinegrave breeches were replaced by narrow knee-breeches (*culotte*) (379, 380, 384), while the short doublet was lengthened to form a knee-length waistcoat with long, narrow sleeves and equipped with large pocket flaps (384) like the coat. It was also the garment worn at home. The stockings were pulled over the breeches at the top (384). After 1690 a cravat was worn round the neck (381, 384), either of lace or of linen with lace at the ends. It was tied tightly so that the lace formed a *jabot* under the chin, where it was fastened with a jewelled clasp or a coloured ribbon. The most beautiful Flemish and Venetian needlepoint lace was used, without scallops, so that it resembled a wide band of insertion.

The new masculine costume gave a firm outline and made the figure look slender and distinguished. Of the superabundance of ribbon loops only a single bow remained on the right shoulder,

but the velvets and gold and silver brocades used in the costume were further embellished with silver and gold embroidery, of which traces still survive in certain types of uniform. In 1662 Louis XIV gave permission for a certain number of his courtiers to wear coats embroidered in gold and silver, the so-called *justaucorps à brevet*, and this was gradually taken up outside the royal circle.

It is typical of the period that the favourite jewel was the cold, sparkling diamond, which was even used for buttons on the resplendent *justaucorps*. Men's shoes had high heels and completely enclosed the feet. The hat was three-cornered (384), with a low crown, and was often not worn on the head but carried under the arm (393).

It is the wig, however, which best symbolizes the age's pursuit of the ornate and the dignified.

The Baroque wig originated in about 1640 as false hair intended to supplement natural hair. As has been noted, the disappearance of the ruff brought in the male fashion for curling locks falling over the shoulders (346, 347), and if nature was not generous enough she was given a helping hand. The first pamphlet against the use of false hair appeared as early as 1642, and was as ineffective as such pamphlets always are. In 1665 Louis XIV appointed forty-eight wigmakers in Paris within a year.

Gradually false hair ousted natural hair. The loose wig worn over the cropped head was often taken off at home and replaced by a skull cap or night cap (383).

Wigs of human hair were extremely expensive, and since they had to be changed it was necessary to have several. As the demand increased, wigs of goathair or horsehair were made, not to mention hair obtained from other and more dubious sources. In 1665 Pepys noted in his diary that he hesitated to put on his new wig as he suspected it was made from the hair of people who had died of the plague.

Towards the end of the seventeenth century the wig was at its most elaborate as the full-bottomed wig. The colour was not, as in the early wigs, fair like a lion's mane, but brown or black. At about the turn of the century the hair was arranged in peaks on either side of the centre parting before flowing over the shoulders in unruly masses of curls, usually longer on the left side than on the right, and continuing down the back as far as the waist. The face was clean-shaven and was made to appear long and thin (*391, 392, 393*).

Women's fashions followed men's in aspiring to a slimmer figure and a more imposing dignity. Their head-dress, the equivalent of the peaks of the full-bottomed wig, rose from the head like a row of organ pipes and provided a background for the curls artfully arranged on the forehead. This was the *fontange* (*382, 385–388*), a construction of silk ribbons, starched lace and linen attached to a small cap at the back of the head. The ends of the frill crowning the head often hung down at the back, while two long ringlets were brought forward over the shoulders—a faint reflection of the vast quantities of hair in the men's wigs (*387*).

Like the men, the women tried to look slender; and as in the Gothic period, their dresses were lengthened into a train. The dress consisted of a bodice, the *taille*, sewn to an open-fronted skirt with a train, the *manteau*, which was looped up at the back and along the front edges so that the underskirt, or *jupe*, could be seen. The drapery at the back was supported on a frame, the first bustle in history. The *manteau* gave the same dignified effect as the voluminous hangings adorning the most important piece of furniture in the home, the large four-poster bed; and the materials and trimmings of these costumes have the same ornate splendour as the patterned velvet and gilded leather covering the chairs and settees.

The richly draped *manteau* was a magnificent garment of heavy satin or velvet lined with satin. Like the man's *justaucorps*, it was removed at home and replaced by a comfortable loose-fitting gown, later called the *contouche* (*388*). The skirt was richly patterned (*387*) or plain and trimmed with horizontal flounces (*falbalas*) (*386*). The bodice was laced across an embroidered stomacher (*385, 386*). The sleeves reached only as far as the elbows, where the lace frills of the chemise appeared (*engageantes*) (*387*). An ornamental apron with a small bib (*385*) was also worn.

Women's costume was décolleté, and for the first time since the classical period the arms were partly bare; but this freedom was counterbalanced by the tightness of the corset. A steel busk half a yard long formed a vertical line from the bust down over the stomach. Laced up in this way, the body took on an immobile, rigid appearance which perfectly suited the formal ceremonial of the age. It must be remembered that this fashion originated in a court where people had to master the art of standing on their feet for hours at a time.

The *fontange* is said to have been named after a certain Mlle Fontange who, for want of anything better while out hunting, tied up her loosened hair with her ribbon- and lace-trimmed garter, much to the delight of her royal lover. Her example was quickly followed by other ladies of the court, and the *fontange* remained in vogue from about 1685 to 1715. It may possibly have originated in some such incident, but its later development as a head-dress which grew taller and taller until about the turn of the century is purely a question of style since, like the *hennin* and the train of the late Gothic period, both were merely a symptom of the tendency to make the female figure appear long and slim.

The *fontange* did not stand up vertically on the head but tilted a little forward. The whole body, from the toes of the high-heeled, embroidered silk shoes to the top of the *fontange*, was similarly inclined, as if pushed forward by the huge quantity of material in the train of the *manteau*.

Late Baroque costume required poise. It had the same richness, dignity and splendour as the other arts and handicrafts of the period.

French Regency

c. 1715–1730

(*Figs. 394–409*)

On the death of Louis XIV in 1715, the Duke of Orleans became Regent during the minority of Louis XV. The transitional style between Baroque and Rococo is known in France, therefore, as 'La Régence'.

The Regency style still retained the strict symmetry of the Baroque, although it was more delicate and refined. The typical decoration of the period is flat, broken ribbon-work—hence 'Ribbon Baroque', the name sometimes given to it. It was also called the 'Bérain style' after the well-known French engraver who contributed so much to its formation. Between the ribbon-work are sprays of bell flowers and the canopies which form such a frequent motif in Chinese art—which brings us to the most important characteristic of the Regency style: the influence of the East. Chinese art had already been known in the seventeenth century but it was not until the Regency that it began to affect style. The black and red lacquer of Chinese furniture was copied, furniture and walls were decorated with imitation Chinese landscapes and figures—called 'Chinoiserie'—and the soft colours of Chinese art were extensively used.

Women's costume during the Regency abandoned the stiffness and formality of late Baroque. The loose-fitting house-coat (*388*), worn by Madame Montespan, among others, during her pregnancies, now appeared in public as the *contouche,* and was worn for strolls or visits whenever formal attire was not required (*395, 397, 404, 408, 409*). Both the train and bustle-effect disappeared, the costume widening in the shape of a funnel towards the hem with the help of a crinoline beneath (*397*). At first the latter was a canvas petticoat supported by metal bands, but it soon gave way to a cotton petticoat over a framework of whalebone. The demand for whalebone increased to such an extent that the Netherlands States General founded a whaling company in 1722 for the sole purpose of providing stiffening for women's hoop petticoats.

The *panier* (wicker basket), as it was called in

France, first appeared in Paris in 1719, having come originally either from England, where it was known as the hoop petticoat, or with the Italian actors brought to France by the Duke of Orleans. It was in fact the Spanish farthingale which the conservative Spaniards had continued to wear ever since the Renaissance (cf. *370, 371*), and which had now been re-introduced. Under the Regency these ankle-length dresses were christened '*robes battantes*' or 'ringing gowns', for the loosely fitting *contouche* stretched conically over the *panier* gave women a bell-like shape, with their small feet in high-heeled silk shoes as the clapper. The *contouche* was open in front like an Asiatic caftan, and had vertical pleats at the back (*397*) named after Watteau, who so often depicted their graceful lines in his paintings. When the Rococo period succeeded the Regency these 'Watteau pleats' were transferred to the gown (*robe*) (*410*).

Conical silhouette of the Regency

The laced bodice of the Baroque period was retained (*405*), but was usually concealed under the wide *contouche*. The cone formed by the dress was surmounted by the head, and to minimize the size of the latter the *fontange* was replaced by a diminutive flat cap perched over a simple coiffure (*397, 398, 408, 409*).

The figures in Watteau's paintings have moved from the stately ornate drawing-rooms of the Baroque period into gardens and parks of a dream-like beauty. The men's dress in his pictures (*396, 399, 403, 406*) is in fact fancy dress, but influenced by the subdued colours of the Regency. If we look at other illustrations of the masculine costume of the period it seems to aim at the same conical sil-

houette (*407*) as the women's. Both the coat and waistcoat were narrow at the shoulders and worn open. The wig decreased in size, and the masses of hair at the back were divided into two parts and tied separately to make the head look smaller. Less lace was used in the cravat, but it was prominently displayed down the vertical opening of the shirt front. The most delicate flower designs were worked in the lace, together with other motifs typical of the French Regency style.

ROCOCO

c. 1730–1770

(*Figs. 410–429*)

The word Rococo is probably derived from *rocaille*, the name given to a decoration of shell-work. It was first used during the French Revolution, and then only to disparage a style the capricious grace of which the Neo-Classicists of the period could not appreciate. Created in France during the 1720s, Rococo is often called the 'Louis Quinze' style after the King who took over the government of France when he came of age in 1723.

The Baroque tradition, after the breathing-space provided by the Regency, continued in a more refined form and indeed reached its culmination during the Rococo period. Rococo was not an architectural style but a type of ornamentation used in interior decoration and furniture design.

The enthusiasm for the art of the Far East reflected in 'Chinoiserie' and the Regency choice of colours persisted throughout the Rococo period, but whereas the Regency had been influenced by its more subdued aspects, Rococo concentrated on its gaiety, playfulness, charm and extravagance, and asymmetrical ornament now appeared in Europe for the first time. Rococo decoration employed asymmetrical shell ornament, S- and C-shaped forms and motifs like bats' wings and palm branches. Straight lines and right angles were systematically avoided. Whereas Regency silverware had made use of the broken line, in the Rococo period the lines were both broken and twisted. Even the shape of the rooms seems to be changed by the ornamentation and the excessive

use of mirrors, which almost eliminate the wall as a containing surface.

In the Rococo style the funnel-shaped *paniers* of the Regency developed into the much fuller dome-shaped hooped petticoat (*418*) over which the material was tightly stretched. The woman's costume had a square neckline and consisted of a skirt (*jupe*) and an open gown (*robe*) (*425*). The sleeves were narrow and reached to the elbows, where the lace flounces (*engageantes*) still appeared (*422, 425, 429*). After 1740 the dome-shaped *panier* was flattened out at the front and back and extended laterally to become what was called a *panier à coudes*. Towards the middle of the century it was sometimes four yards wide at the hem and a lady in *grande toilette* had to sail sideways through doors, the gentleman escorting her having to choose between preceding or following her, since it was impossible to walk at her side and at the same time offer her his hand.

Women were still tightly laced into a corset, a

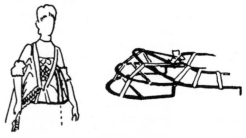

Collapsible panier

fashion to which they had submitted from early childhood (*416*).

The fanciful, asymmetrical festoons of the wall decorations were repeated on the tightly stretched silk of the dress in the form of gathered lace, gathered silk ribbon and especially of the wonderful artificial flowers produced in Italy which made women look like perambulating gardens. The gown was edged with ruching (*425, 429*), the skirt with a single deep gathered flounce (*425*). Large bows on the sleeves matched the ladder-like rows of bows (*échelle*) (*423, 425*) on the breast. A lace ruffle (*423, 425, 429*) was worn round the neck and embroidered silk shoes or high-heeled slippers on the feet. But these flimsy silk shoes were not made for outdoor wear, and the Rococo woman, elegant work of art that she was, was content merely to flirt with nature at a distance (*429*).

The coiffure was set as close to the head as in the Regency period but was now powdered white (*418, 422, 423*), a charming piece of coquetry by which differences of age were obliterated. The powdering was done in a separate room or closet, and the powder, which was wheatmeal, was sprayed upwards so that in falling it could settle evenly on the hair. Less distinguished people powdered their hair on their front doorsteps.

With white-powdered hair went a heavy application of cosmetics, not, as nowadays, in imitation of the natural colours of the face but as a crude form of painting in white and red. It was only ladies of easy virtue who used cosmetics as we do today.

Men's dress followed the silhouette of the feminine costume. The skirts of both the waistcoat and the coat were reinforced with canvas horsehair or paper so that they stood out from the hips in contrast to the narrowness of the shoulders (*413, 415*). Knee-breeches were now fastened over the stockings below the knee with a buckle (*419, 420, 424*).

In spite of the wig, fashion required that the head should appear small, and the hair at the back was gathered into a bag drawn together with a silk bow, the *crapaud* (*415, 424*), from which a silk ribbon, the *solitaire*, was tied round the neck over a plain cravat (*415*). Men's wigs, with the hair drawn back from the forehead, were powdered white like the women's coiffure, and men also used cosmetics. Hats were still three-cornered (*417, 427*). Suits were of silk and, as in women's dresses, the colours harmonized so exquisitely that their effects have never been equalled. They were embroidered with gold, silver or silk thread and spangles, and the lavishness of this embroidery increased towards the middle of the century. The coat was removed at home, and as the waistcoat had lost the long sleeves of the Baroque period and so could not be used as an indoor costume, a comfortable, loose-fitting dressing-gown of silk was introduced (*424*). The lace on the shirt appeared as ruffles at the wrist and as a frill on the chest (*415, 424*). The Rococo period took over the Baroque *justaucorps* from the Regency. This had no collar, but when its skirts became narrower towards the middle of the century a turned-down collar was added (*427*).

The Renaissance tradition comes to an end with the dress of the Rococo period. Both the Renaissance and the Baroque styles had added amplitude and grandeur to the human figure, but the Regency and more especially the Rococo clothed it in a beauty which has never been surpassed. No costume could be more flattering than that worn in the century when men compiled encyclopaedias and women presided over salons, and when Rousseau preached his gospel of the return to nature. Their clothes transformed them into exquisite works of art and conformed perfectly to the spirit of an age which raised its monuments in porcelain and painted its portraits in the coloured dust of the pastel.

Powdered wigs

Louis XVI

c. 1770–1795

(*Figs. 430–459*)

With the discovery halfway through the eighteenth century of Pompeii and Herculaneum, the two ancient cities which had lain buried under a shower of ashes since the eruption of Vesuvius in A.D. 79, Europe developed a passion for classical antiquity. In his history of the fine arts, published in 1755 and the first of its kind, Winckelmann, the German archaeologist, had emphasized the classical qualities of 'noble simplicity and tranquil greatness'. People began to tire of the elegant frivolity of the Rococo and attacked it as the 'art of the brothel'.

This enthusiasm for the antique gradually made itself felt in the style which succeeded the Rococo: neo-Classicism. It falls into several periods: first, the 'Louis Seize' style, then that of the French Revolution or 'Directoire', followed at the beginning of the nineteenth century by the style of the Empire.

The Louis XVI style is an odd mixture of two quite different elements: one the moribund Rococo which had struck deep roots in France, and the other the 'English style' which exemplified the new classicism.

It is characteristic of the Louis XVI style that, although much of its detail such as columns, pilasters and beading was borrowed from the antique, it was presented in the graceful, frivolous manner typical of the Rococo—people were no doubt enthusiastic about antiquity, but it was not an enthusiasm to be taken too seriously. The Louis XVI style has been appositely described as a 'dream of the antique', and in a contemporary pattern book a 'masquerade à la grecque' is actually mentioned. This early form of classicism was not taken any more seriously than that.

The costume of the period shows how French Rococo costume in its final form merged into the new modes which crossed the Channel from England.

Fashion plates, the forerunners of the fashion journals of today, now begin to provide us with a wealth of information.

Men's dress in the 'seventies was the *justaucorps* with large cuffs and pocket flaps (*431*) or the more closely fitting frock coat (*433*). With this was worn a long-skirted waistcoat, knee-breeches (*culotte*), white silk stockings and black shoes with buckles and red heels. The material used was silk, in delicate shades. The hat was still three-cornered and was carried in the hand. The wig, dusted with white or grey powder, was dressed into elegant side curls and usually brushed steeply up from the forehead and gathered into a bag at the back. At home, the *justaucorps* and frock coat were replaced by the more comfortable silk dressing-gown (*436*). In short, the costume was pure Rococo.

In the feminine dress the large *panier* was used only in formal wear. In the négligé which was worn for all other occasions the hoop petticoat had been reduced in size so that it reached only to the knee, and the skirt of the costume (*jupe*) also grew so short that the feet and ankles were visible (*430, 434*). With this went the *caraco* (*430*), a jacket with a pleated back, or the gown (*robe*) was caught up *à la polonaise* in three large loops over the skirt (*432, 434*). Shoes were of silk, with very high heels, and when ladies followed the advice of the French Dr Tronchin and went out to take the air, they carried parasols (*434*) or long walking sticks (*430*).

The lower part of the dress was thus either of an exaggerated width or had been reduced to a kind of dome which had lost contact with the ground. Simultaneously, the head-dress reached such a fantastic size as to be grotesque.

At about the time of Louis XVI's accession in 1774, coiffures were so enormous that it is incredible that women's necks could carry them. As the Baroque period was the heyday of the wig-maker, so the middle 'seventies belonged to the hairdresser. No woman could raise such a structure unaided. The hair was combed up at the sides over a horsehair pad on the crown of the head and attached there with pins and pomade, a looped-up plait and two rows of curls completing the coiffure at the back. Into it the hairdresser worked silk ribbons, feathers, flowers and gauze. But the coiffure could also form a platform for larger objects varying in size from a tulle cap (*432, 434*) to a basket of apples or flowers, or a frigate with all sails set.

Coiffure decorated with ship in full sail

It was sometimes so high that the lady's chin was halfway between her toes and the top of her coiffure, and when travelling in a carriage she had to kneel down to make room for her head.

As it took hours to construct a coiffure like this, it was an expensive luxury which could not be indulged in every day. The rich had their hair taken down and re-arranged once a week, but the less wealthy could only afford to do so every month, and it is not surprising that the vermin which bred there made a 'scratching stick' essential.

Caricature of the large coiffure

Marie Antoinette was both the Queen of France and the Queen of Fashion. She was assisted in the latter function by Rose Bertin, the first fashion designer in history to be mentioned by name, and every month this 'Minister of Fashion' dispatched dolls as mannequins to the courts of Europe, attired both in *grande toilette* and *négligé* as in the Baroque period.

This was the costume of the Rococo period in its final phase. Women's dress had lost the flowing grace and the exquisite poise produced by the contrast between the voluminous hoop petticoat and the small head.

New ideas were however arriving from across the Channel, and for a time England became the acknowledged leader of the world of fashion. For men's clothes, it is a position which she has held ever since.

The costume *à la française* was a permanent party dress, in spite of the fact that people were inspired by Rousseau with a love of nature and by Dr Tronchin with a desire to go for walks.

Englishwoman's costume

The new costume influenced by English fashions was more suitable for the outdoor life. Women's dresses have the same casual charm as the 'English Gardens' which were gradually replacing the formal French gardens with their clipped trees and hedges.

Corsets were still worn, but hoops disappeared and the dress fell softly round the body, held in position by a wide sash with a bow. Instead of an elaborate coiffure, the hair was arranged in loose curls down the back. A small scarf, the *fichu*, went round the shoulders and was crossed on the breast. Décolletage disappeared, and long tight sleeves covered the arms to the wrists. Large, broad-brimmed, Italian straw hats formed a most flattering frame for the charming faces of the women, who were not made up.

The English type of male costume was in fact the costume of our own time, and subsequent modifications have remained superficial. Towards the end of the eighteenth century English tailoring was beginning that long domination of men's styles which has continued up to the present day. In contrast to French Rococo costume of the later period, men's clothes in England were much more restrained and the material heavier. Woollen cloth in bold, practical colours was used, instead of silk and brocade in delicate pastel shades. The coat, often double-breasted, was loose and comfortable, with revers and a high collar. The waistcoat was cut square. This costume began to develop in England while the Rococo style was still flourishing

Englishman's costume

on the Continent, and in essentials it was the costume worn by Englishmen in their portraits, whether painted in Italy (*419, 420*), India (*421*), or at home (*427*). The knee-breeches (*culotte*) of the Rococo were succeeded by pantaloons, the forerunners of the long trousers of today. They were of knitted material, and so long that they reached down into the tight riding boots which replaced shoes and silk stockings. The costume was completed with a tall black hat.

In Germany the English mode became what was called the 'Werther costume', after the hero of Goethe's famous novel published in 1775.

Parisians began to dress *à l'anglaise* in the 1780s. Women wore their hair down their backs in curls dusted with grey powder (*438, 441, 444*). The hoop petticoat was replaced by a small pad at the back

Frenchwoman's costume à l'anglaise

called the *cul de crin* or, outside France, the *cul de Paris*. This produced the same effect as the bustle, and as a counterpoise more and more emphasis was placed on the bust, until the silhouette resembled a pouter-pigeon (*438*). This effect was increased by the *fichu*, at first tied loosely across the breast but gradually rising towards the chin and supported by stays to form the *gorges postiches* or *trompeuse* (*449, 452*). Feminine dress during this period was influenced by sporting and masculine modes, although this may not be immediately obvious. A woman wore a high-crowned man's hat in black on her grey powdered curls, and over her white dress a tightly buttoned man's coat (*444*), the *redingote*, really the English riding coat which had already appeared in France in about 1750 as a man's garment.

There was also a long trailing coat of a similar type, of silk (*447*) or of the striped material so popular·at the time (*440*). The large English straw hats became rather more elaborate in the French version (*441*). One thing should be noted: for the first time dresses were made entirely in white—a colour which was to become of great importance later in the Neo-Classical period (*440, 444, 455*).

In the man's costume *à l'anglaise* fashionable in Paris after 1780 it took some time before shoes and silk stockings (*437, 439*) were discarded for close-fitting riding boots (*443*), and instead of the high-crowned hat one with the brim cocked up at the front and back *à l'androsmane* was often worn (*439*). But plain English clothes were now preferred to silk, and silk embroidery disappeared from men's dress, apparently for good. The 'Werther costume' consisted of short riding boots, tight yellow breeches closed with fly-buttons and

English riding coat

descending into the boots, a blue coat cut short at the waist and with narrow tails, and a high-crowned tapering black hat with a red, white and blue cockade (*450*). This was the masculine costume at the outbreak of the French Revolution on July 14th, 1789.

Two new types of men's dress made their appearance during the Revolution, one on paper, the other actually worn. The latter is associated particularly with the Jacobins, and was derived from various sources: the red 'Phrygian' cap from the galley slaves, a sleeveless, loose-fitting jacket called the *carmagnole* (cf. *428*) from the peasants, and the long, wide trousers from the sailors. Those who adopted it called themselves *sansculottes* in reference to the *culotte* or short knee-breeches worn by the old aristocracy.

The Third Estate had been ordered by the National Assembly to appear in black at their first meeting (which made black fashionable), but the National Assembly showed no enthusiasm for the garb of the *sansculottes* and sponsored instead an entirely new creation called the 'republican costume'. The art of the period was based on Greek and Roman models, the prevailing style was the pseudo-classical, so when David, the leading painter of the Republic, was asked to design this costume the result was a romantic mixture of the antique and Russian boots. As always happens when attempts at dress reform run counter to the natural evolution of costume, the 'republican costume' never got farther than David's sketches. The neo-classical sentiments of the period were to find their expression not in men's clothes but in the feminine costume of the following period.

Directoire

c. 1795–1804
(*Figs. 460–475*)

In 1792 Madame Rose Bertin, Marie Antoinette's 'Minister of Fashion', escaped first to Mainz, then to England. A number of shops in Paris began to supply ready-made clothes to 'citizens' and 'citizenesses', while in England women's dress of the Louis XVI period developed into the 'antique' garb of the New Classicism. The waistline moved up to just below the breasts, as in late Greek and Roman costume, the corset disappeared, and the dress, cut very simply in white or some other quiet colour, was held by a girdle under the breasts. Flat slippers replaced high-heeled shoes, and the body was again supported on the whole of the foot, as in classical times.

While this costume continued to be worn in England (*468, 469*), in Paris it evolved from the 'antique style' into the 'nude style' (*465, 466*). Not only was the corset discarded but the chemise was replaced by flesh-coloured tights (*463*).

Sandals were often worn (*463, 465, 466*). The 'chemise dress', as it was called, had a train, and its flimsy material, muslin, ninon or batiste in white or pastel shades, flowed down loosely from the girdle, giving the impression that the body was growing out of the ground like a tree or a column. The large brim of the straw hat was turned down round the face to form a bonnet, and lengthened in front (*460*).

Draped garments naturally went with the 'antique' costume, and cashmere shawls became an indispensable accessory. People were not 'beautifully dressed' during this period so much as 'beautifully draped'. Ladies carried a bag, the reticule, hanging from the arm by a long silk ribbon.

English Classicising dress

Classical detail had already been used in the Louis XVI period, but now everything in a fashionable room assumed an antique appearance. The bedroom became a bed-temple, and women did their best to look like antique statues in antique costumes. To harmonize with this background their movements had to be graceful and restrained, and the elegant manipulation of the long train (*460, 465, 466*) by the fashionable '*merveilleuses*' became an art in itself.

During this period people talked about being dressed *à la grecque*, and Greece for them was a fabulous country of white marble. But women's dresses had in fact the long-legged, slender appearance of those worn by Roman women, with, in addition, long Gothic trains trailing along the floor *à queue de singe*, like a monkey's tail. The chemise dress was either sleeveless or had short, plain sleeves covering only the shoulders. For a time the bare arms of antiquity were fashionable again.

In about 1795 the Queen of Fashion in Paris

was the beautiful Madame Tallien, called 'Notre Dame de Thermidor'. She appeared at a ball in a chemise dress slit to show her legs in flesh-coloured tights encircled by sandal straps, and wearing jewellery on her neck, arms and bare feet (*463*).

By about 1800 the upper part of the chemise dress became a small separate bodice to which the lower part of the dress was sewn. The neckline was square. At the same time a new garment, the tunic (*473*), was added to the simple feminine costume, which until now had consisted only of the chemise dress. This was worn over the dress or, alternatively, the train ceased to belong to the dress and became a loose accessory of heavy, dark-coloured silk or velvet attached to a small spencer (*474, 475*). This was worn later at Napoleon's court as the court train or *courrobe*.

Women's hair was arranged to imitate the Greek coiffure (*466*), and it was fashionable to change its colour several times a day by donning different wigs, sometimes with ostrich plumes stuck into them (*475*), as on a circus horse. Turbans were also worn.

The male equivalent of the *merveilleuses* of about 1796 were the *incroyables*, whose elegance was judged by the extravagant disarray of their clothes. With their heavy knotted sticks, unruly hair hanging over their ears, jaws hidden in enormous neck-cloths, tight trousers and riding boots, square-cut waistcoats with high waistlines forming a *gilet*, and coats with high, turned-down collars and large lapels, these dandies of the Directoire carried exaggeration of the masculine costume *à l'anglaise* to a point where it became ludicrous. With it was worn either a beaver hat (*467*) or a hat cocked up at the front and back *à l'androsmane* (*461*).

The 'nude style' in France

Empire

c. 1804–1820

(*Figs. 476–507*)

Towards 1800 enthusiasm for the antique became a passion which reached its climax during the Napoleonic Empire. The Romans provided the models for literature, art and oratory, and it was the modern equivalent of the Roman Empire that Napoleon hoped to create.

An attempt was made to revive the spirit of ancient Rome by imitating its architecture, as in the Arc de Triomphe in Paris and the church of the Madeleine, built in the style of a Greek temple. Antique models were everywhere copied.

Napoleon was crowned Emperor in 1804. The influence of the new court on art and architecture led, however, to an over-elaboration of styles.

After Napoleon's Egyptian campaign Egyptian motifs had been used side by side with those of Greece and Rome, e.g. the mahogany furniture of the period was decorated with sphinxes and lions' claws in gilt metal.

The classical influence began to wane during the Empire. The sleeves of women's dresses were puffed and all the fullness was gathered at the back. To encourage the French silk industry, Napoleon banned the importation of Indian muslin, with the result that the flimsy materials of the Directoire were replaced by heavier, more closely woven fabrics like silk and satin.

The train (*476*) was ceasing to be fashionable and had disappeared by 1805 except as the *courrobe* in Napoleon's court. This was a separate garment, very long and wide, and of a different material and colour from the dress itself (cf. *474, 475*). It could be of richly decorated velvet or satin, and was attached to the bodice just below the bust. It is still worn today as part of ceremonial court costume.

In women's dress the waistline remained just below the breasts all through the period. The outer garment, which was cut on the same lines, was either the short spencer with long sleeves or the long *redingote* (*477, 485, 497, 501, 504*).

Shawls were still worn, and the fashion plates show how they were manipulated. In colour they contrasted effectively with the predominant white of the dress, and were either draped loosely behind the back (*478*), trailed along the ground (*488*), or used to accentuate a graceful pose (*502*). They were carried in the hand (*491*), over the arm (*480*), or arranged as a background for the white dress

Courrobe of Napoleon's Court

(*503*). With the tendency for dresses to fit more closely, the shawl lost its importance as a graceful accessory and was supplemented by a small triangular shoulder scarf or *fichu*. This did not encourage classical poses, but whether worn loose (*494*) or crossed over in front and tied behind (*491*), it covered the low décolletage. The bare arms of antiquity were hidden in long coloured gloves (*482*) which were gradually replaced by long narrow sleeves emerging from the small puffed sleeves on the upper arm (*495*).

The dress, having lost its train, began to grow shorter and to show more of the feet and the flat shoes.

Having reached a peak of plainness, it now began to be trimmed again, and embroidered garlands of flowers (*491, 502*), frills at the hem (*498*), appliqué work with a serrated edge in the same material as the dress (*dents de loup*) (*490*), and ruching (*486, 499*) were much in evidence. They all had one thing in common in that they emphasized the horizontal line at the expense of the vertical folds.

This type of dress in its final phase had a boat-shaped neckline and completely exposed the feet (*507*).

The head-dress most characteristic of the period was still the poke-bonnet with its projecting brim completely hiding the face (*480, 494*), although small hats and turbans (*497, 498*) were also worn.

Men's costume saw the development of what ultimately became the long trousers of today. Both leather breeches and riding boots (*484, 487, 500*), as well as the knitted tights (*505*) which had been worn in England during the Directoire (cf. *470*,

471) gave way in about 1815 to the long wide trousers which the *sansculottes* of the Revolution had not succeeded in making fashionable (*506*). This was the final stage in the creation of modern male dress. Knee-breeches were now worn only with Court dress (*493*).

In England this was the period of 'Beau' Brummell, known to posterity as the perfect type of the well-dressed gentleman. Between 1800 and 1816 English society was dominated by his good taste in clothes. He taught his clumsier contemporaries not only how to tie a complicated cravat but an entirely new conception of elegance. More than anyone else, he was the inventor of the idea that to be well dressed is to be unostentatious, and that it is not the trimmings that make the suit but the excellence of the cut and the way it is worn.

The Nineteenth Century

c. 1820–1870
(*Figs. 508–598*)

The nineteenth century was an age of revivals. No original style was created, but as much more was known of the styles of the past than ever before, architects and designers were able to draw on this rich source of inspiration. In no other century was there so much talk of style; and no other century seems to us more lacking in it.

The background to the period is the unprecedented economic development which, beginning shortly after 1800, ushered in the age of capitalism and the machine. Until then handwork had been supreme, especially in the arts, with which costume must be classed. Clothing had hitherto been made by individual craftsmen and artists whose work, both in quality of workmanship and beauty of design, far surpassed anything that was produced later.

It was a period in which the teaching of the art schools was confined to the 'fine arts', leaving the applied arts and handicrafts to look after themselves. At the same time the class with money to spend changed in character; it became larger, less discriminating and more willing to accept imitations instead of the genuine article.

The revival of earlier styles is already apparent

in the neo-Classicism of the Directoire and Empire periods. First the art of ancient Rome had been copied, then, under Napoleon, that of Egypt, until eventually influences poured in not only from the different historical periods but from every part of the world as well.

With the reaction against the Empire style in about 1820 other styles appeared, as unlike those of Egypt and Rome as possible. England revived the Gothic, the rest of Europe the Rococo. While the Gothic did not affect costume, Rococo strongly influenced both costume and furniture.

It was, however, a middle-class imitation of the eighteenth century court style. Undulating curves replaced the straight lines of Empire furniture, and the wood used was now carved, polished mahogany with heavy padding and covers of dark woollen material often patterned with large bouquets of flowers. Upholstery was all the rage by about 1840. The wood was almost completely concealed, and instead of dark woollen covers, wine-red or bottle-green plush was used, while rows of tassels and fringes appeared everywhere on curtains, portières, sofas and chairs and as edging to table tops, tablecloths and whatnots.

In the sitting-rooms of the period, the oil lamp shed its glow on a middle-class idyll presided over by solid commonsense. But it was also the age of romanticism when, nurtured on such writers as Sir Walter Scott (1771–1832), George Sand (1804–1876) and Alexandre Dumas (1802–1870), the imagination took wing in search of adventure in past centuries and far-away lands.

The feminine costume of the Empire, which was low-cut, high-waisted, plain in front and gathered into folds behind, underwent a change. Under the Empire, dresses had already become shorter at the hem and were closed round the neck, but now the girdle moved down from below the breasts to where a woman is slimmest, at the waist. The immediate result was the return of the corset. Below the waist the skirt grew wider, at first only moderately, but with the folds from the back distributed all round.

Appliqué trimming continued to be used for a time, and a great deal of work went into trimming dresses of fairly cheap material with ruching and ruffles arranged in three or four horizontal bands to make them stand out at the hem. These decorations could be narrow (508, 511, 520), wide (519, 521), or arranged in a heavy Greek key pattern 5516). An enormous amount of time was also spent on embroidering broderie anglaise by hand (17).

The poke-bonnet was still in fashion, although it now looked more like a hat than a bonnet (516). Flat shoes also continued to be worn, but became square at the toes and were fastened by cross-lacing up the legs. Although dresses were closed round the neck and had begun to spread over the shoulders in wide collars (508, 516, 517), the shawl was still used (516, 517).

The tendency to widen the skirt over an increasing number of petticoats, sometimes as many as seven or eight, was accompanied by greater width at the top. It was not, however, the width of the shoulders themselves which was increased. The feminine dress of the period seems to do its utmost to conceal the fact that a woman's arms are joined to her body at the shoulders. The sloping shoulder-line produced by the large falling collar was now further exaggerated, the collar increasing in size until it formed a sort of roof (523, 530) over the greatly distended sleeves. At first very wide at the top, they were called 'leg-of-mutton' sleeves (gigots) (519), but after 1830 the width dropped to

the elbows (523, 530) and the armhole moved from its normal position to halfway down the upper arm, so that women appeared to have very short arms on a wide, rounded bust (523, 530). The movement of the arms was thus restricted, and even in the riding habit the armholes were so awkwardly placed that the arms could not be raised freely (529, 533).

The combination of wide skirt, wasp-waist and exaggerated bust produced the hour-glass silhouette.

The hour-glass silhouette

Masculine costume underwent a similar transformation. Although the long trousers, coat and waistcoat had by now become permanent features of men's dress, they still had to undergo a number of modifications before they became the suit which is worn today. The masculine silhouette echoed the woman's for a considerable time.

In the long trousers of the period a strap was sewn under the instep, and they were so full at the top that they added width to the hips. Both the coat, tailcoat and overcoat were tailored to fit very closely (509, 522) and had leg-of-mutton sleeves (509, 515) joined to the coat just below the shoulders. The cape (512) or the long shawl collar (525) gave the shoulders a rounded appearance. If the cut of the coat did not produce a narrow waist, a corset or 'basque belt' was worn which pinched it into something approaching the wasp-waist of the feminine mode.

With the rounded shoulders, narrow waist and wide hips of the masculine costume, one can understand how the famous author who wrote under the name of George Sand could look so like a young man when, on her mother's advice and in order to get about Paris more easily, she exchanged the inconvenient petticoats of the period for the more practical attire of a man. A very tall top hat was always worn, except with court dress, when the hat was cocked at the front and back (*518*).

Men wore side-whiskers and curls (*510*) corresponding to the asymmetrically arranged hair of the women with ringlets at the temples (*511, 520*).

The hour-glass shape of the grown-ups was repeated in the skirted blouse (*535, 536*) and long trousers of the boys' costume (*527*), while girls wore a shorter version of their mothers' dresses with a wide skirt over a number of petticoats, large sleeves widest at the elbows, and sloping shoulders. But the girls too began to wear long trousers of a sort in the so-called 'pantalets'.

The light dresses in soft pastel shades of the Directoire and Empire periods had encouraged women to pay more attention to bodily hygiene than had been the case during the Rococo period. They now not only changed their clothes and washed more frequently but in about 1800 began to wear drawers, which until then had rarely been part of the feminine wardrobe.

Women apparently felt that, having at last acquired this masculine garment, they had better display it. In the girl's costume it was shown quite openly as two loose trouser legs reaching down to the ankles and either open (*524, 535*) or gathered in (*526*) at the bottom.

From about 1835 the upholsterer took over interior decoration from the cabinet maker, to create what in England was called the Early Victorian period and in Europe the New Rococo. The basic shape of furniture was concealed under upholstery, tassels and fringes, and costume developed along similar lines.

Women's costume ceased to be as light as a ballet dress. The ankle-length skirt, revealing the feet in flat shoes with cross lacing, was lengthened to the ground and the width at the elbows reduced. The fullness of the sleeves descended lower and lower until it disappeared altogether. The natural lines of the upper part of the body were revealed again so that a modelled bust appeared to rest on a dome-shaped pedestal; the hour-glass silhouette gave place to the tea-cosy silhouette.

Dresses now hid cloth boots and white cotton stockings.

The outer garment was at first a loose coat with large sleeves (*547, 548*), but later became a waisted coat with narrow sleeves (*562, 564*). Under the poke-bonnet the hair fell in short ringlets on either side of the face (*541, 552, 554*) or was combed straight down over the ears from the centre parting (*542, 559, 560*). The bell-shaped skirt was distended by several petticoats worn one over the other, and to make it even fuller the petticoats were stiffened. This was done in various ways. Over a flannel petticoat came first a petticoat padded with horsehair, then one of cotton stiffened with braid, then one with flounces of horsehair, and finally, under the dress, one or two petticoats of starched muslin.

The weight of so many petticoats eventually became intolerable and in about 1850, for the third time in history, a frame was introduced to hold out the dress. This was called the crinoline, a name originating from the French word for horsehair padding, *crin*. The crinoline was a framework of bamboo, whalebone or metal hoops suspended from tapes and increasing in width towards the hem. It did away with some of the petticoats and in the next decade was the indispensable basis of every dress.

The crinoline dress

With the crinoline came the possibility of widening the lower part of the tea-cosy silhouette, and this was exploited to the full. It also led to the replacement of the coat by a large shawl, square in shape but folded into a triangle with the point hanging down the back (*573–575*).

As in the Rococo period, the head was now made to look as small as possible in contrast to the huge crinoline. The poke-bonnet, already much reduced in size, had served its purpose and was replaced by a small *capote* hat (*590, 597*) which, like the poke-bonnet, was tied under the chin with silk ribbon.

In the New Rococo style the lower part of the dress was divided by horizontal lines corresponding to the ruching and garland trimmings of the Rococo period. This began before the crinoline became fashionable, when the lower part of the dress might consist of several layers of different lengths, or there might be flounces at the hem (*541, 551, 553*). With the introduction of the crinoline the whole of the bell-shaped skirt was trimmed with an increasing number of horizontal frills or flounces (*582, 597*). Crêpe dresses are reported to have had fifteen, organdie dresses eighteen and tarlatan dresses as many as twenty-five!

The effect of the flouncing on the skirt was repeated in the *bertha* round the shoulders (*582*) and spread also to the sleeves, which gradually became funnel shaped, with undersleeves of white tulle attached to the elbow with elastic (*590, 597*).

The number of flounces continued to increase. In 1859 the Empress Eugénie wore a white satin ball-gown trimmed with 103 flounces of tulle.

The Empress Eugénie, who was Spanish by birth, was married to Napoleon III in 1853. One of the most beautiful women in Europe, she was the leader of fashion during the period and her patronage made Worth, her couturier, famous. In 1858 he opened his salon and became the founder of *haute couture* in Paris. His customers included not only the Empress and her court— whose favourite colour, incidentally, was white—but actresses and the demi-monde. It was during this period that the demi-monde became even more important than the court in launching new fashions.

The materials for women's dresses were expensive. Silk and satin were worn at any time of the day or night, as were shot taffeta, silk damask, brocade and, most enchanting of all, watered silk. For balls and summer wear very light materials such as crêpe-de-chine, gauze, muslin, barège and tarlatan were used, and from 1852 gauze woven with two differently coloured threads. When wearing these light crinoline dresses trimmed with flounces women were rightly compared to floating clouds. The material was not as expensive as silk or satin, but the dress cost just as much, partly because of the enormous amount of work that went into it, and partly because it could be worn only a few times before it lost its freshness and therefore its elegance. When the sewing machine came from America to Europe in the 'forties, the labour of making these flounces was greatly diminished.

The crinoline dress reached its peak towards the end of the 'fifties and then declined. It was either shortened or changed its shape, like the whalebone petticoat of the Rococo period. It became oval instead of round, with greater fullness at the back, and the hoops appeared as it were to slip downwards; or it was shortened to show the feet. The short crinoline was a transient phenomenon of the 'sixties, when both the coloured petticoats underneath and the feet with their cloth boots became visible. Stockings were also coloured instead of white. Dresses became so gaudy that they were called *genre canaille*, and indeed they do leave an extraordinary impression of vulgarity. They may have been a result of that remarkable cult of the demi-monde introduced by Dumas *fils* with his play *La Dame aux Camélias*, which showed the *grande cocotte* in a romantic light and made her interesting even to ladies of the highest respectability.

At the beginning of the period men's dress was very tight-fitting, with a shaped waist like that of the feminine costume (*543, 549, 555, 558, 563*) and a more normal shoulder width. The top hat was obligatory, but in 1848 the beaver hat was supplanted by the silk hat. The hair was worn in a bob with curls all round the head (*538, 545, 555, 558*). Beards usually formed a fringe round the face (*563*), but later side-whiskers were worn with a moustache and 'Imperial'.

At about the time when women began to wear crinolines, the masculine dress became uniform in colour. The term 'a suit of clothes' had been invented. In 1860 standing collars and cravats were replaced by starched collars and ties (*593, 594*), and different suits were worn for different occasions. The top hat was no longer the only kind of headwear for men, and the bowler hat appeared (*591, 594*).

Boys wore the bowlers (*581*) and long trousers of their fathers (*556, 581*); the wide-skirted petticoats of the girls repeated the lines of the woman's dress (*540, 595*). Pantalets were now on the way out, having become so narrow that they no longer provided a camouflage for the legs (*557*).

The christening robes still worn by babies were created during the neo-classical period. If you look at the contemporary christening robe carefully you will see that it is still the high-waisted woman's dress of the Directoire and Empire which, in a diminutive form, has survived unaffected by the changes in adult costume (*588*).

c. 1870–1890

(*Figs. 599–614*)

During the last quarter of the century the imitation of styles became a confusion of styles, each of which was applied to a different purpose. Studies and dining-rooms were in the Renaissance style, smoking-rooms in the Oriental style which had been introduced by the sensational success of the Moroccan and Turkish sections of the 1851 Exhibition in London and which led to the adoption of divans and potted palms. Girls' rooms and ladies' boudoirs were, however, still decorated in light, soft colours. Simultaneously, old national and traditional peasant styles began to be exploited.

This turbulent mixture of styles was regarded as artistic broadmindedness and was supposed to give period charm to buildings and articles of everyday use.

Cosiness in the home was achieved by means of thick, draped curtains and door-hangings which shut out light and air, while heavy upholstery gave the chairs, sofas and stools an elephantine immobility. Tassels are the typical ornament of the period which reached its climax in Makart's 'studio style' of about 1875, with its bunches of lacquered bulrushes, wax flowers and peacocks' feathers. Table covers were so long that they touched the floor, concealing the fact that a table has legs, and rooms were crammed with knickknacks and cheap mass-produced articles which had no connection with art or fine craftsmanship.

The material in women's dresses was cut up into small pieces which were then sewn together again, like the material for curtains and portières before it was hung round the doors and windows. Folds were draped across pleats in the same dress, and glossy material used with dull, silk with velvet (*600, 602*). Especially popular, as giving a very subtle effect, was the juxtaposition of several materials of the same colour.

The mode for women's dresses during these years was thus the same as for furniture. Furniture in the 'Renaissance style', as it was called, continued to be manufactured after imitation Rococo had gone out of fashion. No distinction was made in the trade between Renaissance and Baroque, and it was the *manteau* and *fontange* of the late Baroque period which reappeared in women's costume as the bustle-dress and the *capote* hat. But, as happened when the Louis XVI style replaced the Rococo, there was no abrupt transition from the crinoline to a costume which followed the natural lines of the body; instead, the padding was retained and transferred to the back, with increased emphasis on the bust. In the Louis XVI period this effect was obtained by means of the *cul de crin*, a small pad at the back, and the *fichu* which later developed into the *trompeuse* (cf. *438*). Now the bust was pushed up by a tight corset which at the same time forced out the abdomen a little. At the back was an odd contraption called the bustle. Beginning as a small pad of horsehair or a few flounces of starched linen, it soon developed into a framework of horse-shoe shaped bars suspended horizontally from tapes so that it hung at the back, under the dress but over the petticoats, like a kind of bird-cage. With this as a support the overskirt was draped up as imaginatively as the portières and curtains hung by the upholsterer.

The bustle was in vogue from 1870 to 1876, and again for a time in the 'eighties. In the intervening period it disappeared, but skirts were still caught-up behind and wrapped tightly round the lower part of the body, making it so difficult to move that the knees seemed to be tied together.

Out of these draperies the hips, waist and bust emerged with a magnificent flourish which owed much to corsetry and padding. A long row of buttons down the front emphasized the lines of the figure. For social occasions dresses were sleeveless and décolleté.

In the 'eighties the bustle came back into favour. At first the natural lines of the hips were still revealed (*600, 603*), but soon the drapery gained in bulk and the skirt over which the overdress was draped became looser to give greater freedom of movement (*606–608*).

A skirt with a bustle was worn with a tailored jacket (*609*), and the bustle was even retained in skating costume (*611*). It did not disappear until the end of the 'eighties (*613, 614*).

During these years the morning coat (*599*) and the frock coat (*610*) became part of the masculine wardrobe, as did the suit specially made for sum-

The bustle of the 'seventies

mer wear and worn with a straw hat or 'boater' (*605*). In sporting dress, the knickerbockers were of the same cut as those in boys' suits (*604*).

c. 1890–1900

(*Figs. 615–622*)

By 1890 the bustle had disappeared, leaving behind it a certain amount of residual drapery in the skirt (*615*). This did not, however, survive very long. The skirt became smooth in front with its main fullness concentrated at the back, and the sleeves were widest at the armhole to emphasize the shoulders, which were still held stiffly, as when the bustle was worn (*616*). The leg-of-mutton sleeves and the hour-glass silhouette of about 1825 (*617–619* and cf. *517, 519*) had come back into fashion.

Halfway through the 'nineties a new corset appeared which changed the outline of the stiff, rather formal carriage of the feminine figure. In front it had a vertical steel stay, the *blanchet*, which eliminated the abdomen as if by magic and shifted the fullness of the figure upwards into the protruding bust and backwards behind the hips. It gave women a curious S-shaped, sway-back figure, with the bust apparently carried in advance of the lower part of the body. The corset was called simply the *sans ventre* or the *gegen das Kind* (Anti-Baby), leaving no doubt of its purpose. The dress was

high-necked, except for evening wear, and had a high collar stiffened by boning. The trumpet-shaped skirt was sewn in panels flaring out towards the hem.

An odd form of coquetry was associated with the underclothes. These high-necked, long-sleeved dresses could conceal marvels of rustling silk in petticoats trimmed with flounces and lace and threaded with silk and velvet ribbon. Their presence was betrayed by the seductive 'frou-frou' of the silk, or they could be glimpsed when the skirt was raised, as was often necessary in the street. A whole world of meaning could be conveyed by the way the dress was held up, from a prudish snub to the most daring flirtatiousness.

Women also took over the masculine three-piece tailored suit (*616*) to form a costume consisting of skirt, jacket and shirt-blouse; and the blouse influenced the bodice of dresses towards a greater fullness of material in front. The bodice was smothered in every conceivable kind of trimming—lace, false buttons, frills, etc. (*622*). With the arrival of tailor-made costumes worn with different blouses, women's garments were mass-produced in standard sizes by the ready-made dress trade, so that their clothing lost much of its individuality.

The corset was a danger to health. This is true of all corsets, but the one which produced the sway-back carriage gave rise to vociferous demands for its replacement by something more healthy and practical, and this in turn led to a movement for reform called the 'anti-fashion campaign'.

Actually, it was a fight which had begun much earlier. In 1851 an American, Amelia Bloomer, had demonstrated in London a revolutionary costume consisting of a jacket and short skirts over long,

Amelia Bloomer's   *'Bloomers'*
'reform' costume   *worn for gymnastics*

baggy, Turkish trousers. The 'Bloomer Costume' caused a great stir and societies were formed for and against it. But women were just starting to go in for physical exercises, and 'bloomers', as the long, Turkish trousers were called, became part of their costume for gymnastics.

Amelia Bloomer had her successors. In 1867 a doctor suggested abolishing the corset and suspending the crinoline from braces in order to transfer the weight of the dress from the waist to the shoulders. In 1886, when bustles were being worn, another doctor suggested replacing the corset with what he called a *chemilette*, that is, combinations of wool or cotton under a 'hygienic' camisole. He expressly emphasized that if a woman felt she missed the support of the corset, the camisole could be made of stiff material. Two short petticoats and a pair of long, wide, flannel drawers similar to bloomers were to be buttoned on to it,

Attempts at reform, 1867 and 1886

and on top of all this came the dress. The fashionable costume at the time was the bustle-dress, which was inconceivable without the corset as a foundation. The only dress which could be worn over this underwear was a long, shapeless, tunic frock, the 'reform sack', which, naturally enough, excited the enthusiasm of only a few fanatics. In the long run fashion won, and dress reform was achieved on entirely different lines.

In England a reaction against the imitation and mixture of styles had set in with the formation of the Pre-Raphaelite Brotherhood in 1848, the leader of which was the painter Dante Gabriel Rossetti. Its members banded themselves together against the vulgarity of their period and sought to rejuvenate the decorative arts by reviving the methods and outlook of the medieval craftsman.

In 1862 William Morris, with Rossetti's assistance, founded the firm of Morris, Marshall, Faulkner and Co. with this aim in mind. The machine was blamed for the decline of style in the nineteenth century, and Morris held the view that if the artist of today worked with the same devotion as the craftsmen of the Middle Ages, everything inside the walls of a house would once more be beautiful. He maintained that the shape of an object must be adapted to its purpose, and that handicraft was the only way out of the impasse in which the Victorians found themselves.

To meet this new interest in handicraft, art museums were built like the Victoria and Albert Museum in London, and schools for teaching handicraft made it possible for students not only to study the craftsmanship of the past but to give the same quality to the articles which they made themselves.

This was a literary and artistic movement which

ran counter to the conventions of the age. Its influence on women's dress was towards allowing the material to fall loosely and naturally round the body, but only a few unco-ordinated efforts were made in this direction.

Meanwhile, technological and industrial development in Europe continued undisturbed. In 1851 the Crystal Palace with its dome of steel and glass was erected in London; in 1869 the naked steel girders of the Eiffel Tower rose over the Paris Exhibition. The machine age gave to these steel constructions a beauty of their own, but it was a beauty which at the time failed to appeal to the artist, whose brain creates those revolutions of taste from which new period styles emerge.

The first artist who did not find his inspiration in the art and handicraft of the past was Henry van de Velde, a Belgian. Although to some extent he continued the work begun by William Morris, when he became prominent in the 'nineties he brought with him much that was entirely new. He saw in the machine and in the soaring curves of structures in steel a repetition of the supple lines of natural forms in flowers and foliage, and tried to transfer them to furniture and interior decoration. But another tradition, an influence from the East, also contributed to the style he created.

In 1850 Japan was at last opened to Europeans, and Japanese woodcuts used as packing for Japanese goods exported to Europe created a sensation among the artists of Paris. The Japanese use of colour and line was a revelation, for as the lines were not drawn with pen or pencil but with a soft brush, they varied in thickness. The dynamic, flowing line of Japanese art was repeated in Van de Velde's ornamentation.

Design for a concert gown by Van de Velde

In his work we find the first hint of what today is called 'streamlining'. His furniture and his whole treatment of line caused enormous excitement when, as *Art Nouveau*, it was shown at the Paris Exhibition of 1900. The movement spread to Germany, where it was called the '*Jugendstil*' or 'Youth style'.

Van de Velde was also interested in women's dress and his fluid ornamentation recurs in designs for a number of loose 'reform sacks'. But his sketch for a concert gown is much closer to the costume fashionable during his day, and in fact the sway-back feminine figure of the 'nineties with the long, trumpet-shaped skirt swinging in spirals round the feet (*621–624*) is much more closely related to *Art Nouveau* or the *Jugendstil* than are his own experiments in dress reform. During these years women did in fact have a streamlined appearance (*627–629*).

The Twentieth Century

1900–1970
(Figs. 623–689)

The fashionable costume of the first decade of the twentieth century, while stubbornly resisting all attempts at reform whether on grounds of convenience or health, gave expression to the *Art Nouveau* spirit.

Not until some time thereafter was the corset abolished, and then not by the efforts of dress-reformers but simply by becoming superfluous.

Women at last reached the stage when they were no longer hampered by their clothes. This happy state of affairs was not achieved, however, against the prevailing fashion, but evolved out of it.

By about 1910 the trumpet-shaped skirt began to close round the feet to form the hobble skirt. Women grew taller and slimmer, although they retained the sway-back posture, the ample bust and enormous hats (*630*).

The reformers were also interested in men's dress. In 1890 Hans Jäger, with his slogan 'Wer weise wählt Wolle' ('The wise man chooses wool'), had tried to reform underwear. He also tried to introduce a new type of coat based on the military jacket and designed to protect the chest. At that time attempts to reform both men's and women's underwear seem to have been mostly concerned with the problem of producing clothing which was sufficiently warm.

The real reaction against the nineteenth century mixture of styles began shortly before the first World War. As a result of the various attempts to create something different, a new style arose which was just as epoch-making as other new styles have been throughout the centuries, although we may perhaps find this difficult to appreciate as we are still so close to it.

Hitherto a campaign had been waged against the machine and all it stood for. Its products had been camouflaged and smothered with applied ornament; new materials were hidden under an alien veneer. But it gradually began to dawn on people that machines could produce things of beauty. The efficiency of the machine created a demand for efficiency in the various accessories of daily life, and the potentialities of the new materials became apparent.

Architects and furniture designers sought to break away from superfluous ornament and the imitation of hand-craftsmanship, and stripped their designs down to basic forms. The criterion was no longer that an object should be pretty to look at but that it should achieve beauty by working well and fulfilling its purpose efficiently.

These new ideas were soon applied to women's dress. The first costumes to show their influence now seem very remote, but difficult as it is to believe that the clothes we wear today derive from those of immediately before and during the first World War, this is in fact the case, although the period was perhaps less notable for its foreshadowing of things to come than for its decisive break with things past.

The new mode was announced by a Danish fashion magazine in June 1913 as 'The Revolution in Fashion: the new Botticelli figure'. 'The new and startling thing,' it stated, 'even at first slightly repulsive, is that the abdomen must protrude

The Botticelli figure   *Botticelli's feminine type*

slightly. It is to be hoped that ladies will not hesitate to adopt the new Botticelli figure, for the sake of their health if for nothing else. The new fashion will delight all admirers of the female form.'

'It is apparently a superstition,' the paper continued, 'that clothes must fit to the body. On the contrary, the more the material is pulled, draped and gathered, and the more it obscures the lines of the figure, the better.' The 'fine figure' produced by the corset had been declared obsolete.

The silhouette referred to (*631*) bears only a superficial resemblance to a Botticelli painting (cf. *269*), and the new mode was not inspired by the Renaissance but by Japan. Just as the decorative art of the French Regency and Rococo periods had been strongly influenced by Chinese art, so the influence of Japan is apparent today in the way we arrange our homes, in the harmony between house and garden, and in many of the materials we use. It also affected costume. The feminine silhouette now took on the lines of the Japanese kimono, a style which was first used in women's fur coats. After 1913 its influence was apparent in the characteristic drapery, the simplicity of the cut, and the fact that the sleeves were not distinct tubes but extensions of the body of the dress.

The draped effect of the kimono is reflected in the way the material of the dress is gathered round the body from behind (*632*, *633*), and the bodice is likewise cut kimono-fashion (*636*). All the morning gowns, dressing-gowns, etc., of the previous period were now replaced by a 'kimono', which was usually made precisely like the Japanese kimono, with long, hanging, bag-shaped sleeves and in materials with Japanese patterns.

The waist moved up to just below the breasts (*634, 636*), and at last the corset disappeared, the abdomen and hips being enclosed in a wide elastic belt which left the bust free.

The dream of even the most fanatical dress reformers had now been realized, but the corset was not abandoned without a struggle. Reactionaries of the old school raised their voices in praise of the posture produced by the corset and in condemnation of the 'slack, corsetless youth of today'.

The new fashion also meant the end of skirts in the old sense. The lower part of the dress was tightly draped in a sheath round the legs, which were partly revealed by a slit front. For evening dress what was called the 'mermaid train' was worn (*636*). The abdomen was emphasized by posture (*633*), by looping-up (*636*), or by Poiret's 'half-crinoline', a short, bell-shaped overdress falling from the high waist (*634*).

Poiret was the leading dress designer of the day. His creations, shown at parties in his Paris villa in a setting of Oriental splendour, were greatly influenced by the colour schemes of the Russian ballet, which also affected other Paris dress designers like Paquin (*633*).

The development of this new style was completed after the first World War. The severely practical conception of a house as a machine for living in and not as a monumental frame round the lives of its inmates was put forward by the leading architect of the period, the French-Swiss Charles Edouard Jeanneret, better known as Le Corbusier. By the middle 'twenties this had led to the idea of Functionalism.

Simultaneously, a practical and Functionalist woman's dress made its appearance. First, the draped lines influenced by the Japanese kimono disappeared. Dresses and coats fell loosely round the body from the waist, which remained high, and they showed a marked tendency to become shorter and to reveal the fact that a woman, like a man, walks on two legs (*637, 638*). Then the 'straight line' became all the rage. Faint traces of it had appeared earlier in sports costumes (*635*) while they were still long, but now the length of the dress was much diminished. By 1924 women's costume had developed into a short, absolutely straight dress, hanging from the shoulders and usually sleeveless, with the waist round the hips. The bare arms of antiquity had returned (*646*). The curves of the body were completely ignored, the female form being presented as a sort of tube without either hips or breasts, and with their usual remarkable adaptability women actually managed to create this effect (*639, 641, 643, 645, 646, 647*).

The low waist marked the top of the legs, and more and more of the legs, clad in light silk stockings, was exposed, until the dress reached its minimum length in 1928 (*645*).

Simultaneously, the Eton crop and bobbed hair appeared (*645, 646*). It was a bizarre idea to remove what has always been regarded as a woman's 'crowning glory', and the result was *la garçonne*, a youthful figure of indeterminate sex. The feminine

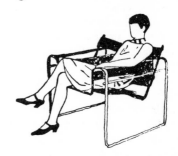

Short dress, silk stockings and Eton crop

dress of the period was clearly an expression of the sober, practical style based on a consideration of how things function—houses, furniture and the human body. Its cut was the same for all occasions, the difference between day and evening gowns being indicated only by the degree of elegance and workmanship in the materials.

In about 1930, however, evening gowns grew longer, first at the back, then all the way round. But although long dresses came back for evening wear, they did not conceal much compared with the long dresses of other periods. The material was cut on the bias, i.e. the elasticity of the weave was used, and followed the shape of the hips and thighs as far as the knee (*648, 649*), thus revealing all the feminine curves which the 'straight line' had concealed.

At the same time, evening gowns developed a type of décolletage unknown in any previous period. They became backless (*648, 649, 653*).

This distinction between short day dresses and long evening gowns has persisted ever since. The length of day dresses varies—they were longest in 1948 when the long-skirted dress of the New Look

(*660, 661*) was launched by Dior, the leading dress designer in Paris today.

In 1946 backless evening gowns, relying on the elasticity of the bias material, were replaced by strapless evening gowns with very full skirts (*657*), and in recent years short evening gowns have appeared with deep V-necklines (*668*). At the same time a tendency to emphasize the bust has replaced the emphasis on shoulder width. But it is outside the scope of this book to describe modern trends in dress from year to year. All these slight modifications in costume are only variations of that 'functional' style which still dominates our fashions.

The contribution of our own period to the history of costume can now be summarized. The basic form of the man's suit had been established just before or during the French Revolution. Its lines have varied in sympathy with those of women's dress, but in form it has remained substantially the same. Various new garments have been added to it, and it has been considerably simplified for sport and holiday wear. The tailored suit has, however, retained a certain amount of padding, and vestigial remains like buttons, button-holes and pockets, which have long lost their purpose, often show how the garment originated. Improved heating giving a constant summer temperature indoors all the year round has not yet resulted in lighter indoor and heavier outdoor suits for men, as has been the case with women. But the construction of the man's suit is so practical (*670, 679*) that women have adopted it (*669*). Formal dress, e.g. the tail coat and top hat (*656*), is disappearing from young people's wardrobes, for it is expensive to buy, requires care and attention and must be worn with a dignity which is quite alien to the present day. A simplified dinner jacket without a waistcoat often replaces the tail coat as evening wear. With all this, however, it is true to say that in general men's dress has changed less during the last 150 years than women's, which has reflected the change of styles much more plainly.

The influence of the style of our own period on women's costume can be clearly demonstrated. The greatest achievement of Functionalism is that it has made women's dresses short, and they remain short in spite of long evening gowns. Moreover, it has made women's costume much more varied than men's. In Europe a skirted dress has been the only possible garment for women from the days of the ancient Greeks almost to our own

time, but now trousers have been adopted, for sportswear since 1900, for indoor wear since the 'thirties (*655*), and nowadays for work and holidays (*671, 672*). Women have thus taken over the most practical forms of male dress while at the same time retaining their own skirted dress. Their wardrobe today is much more varied than at any other period in history.

A woman's costume, then, is both practical and healthy, and does not hamper movement. She need no longer begin dressing in the morning, as in the days when elaborate corsets were worn and stays had to be tightened every hour so that she could squeeze into her dress for the evening.

As new building materials have given rise to new building techniques, so within the last thirty years new dress fabrics have been produced to meet the demand for simple, 'functional' clothes.

At the turn of the century it was often said that everyday dress should resemble tights in allowing freedom of movement while being neither too constricted nor too heavy. The present period uses for this purpose rubber and elastic, material cut on the cross, and knitted fabrics. Women's clothes are both *close-fitting* and *elastic*; they allow unrestricted movement while at the same time clinging to the lines of the body.

Our clothing is *cheap* compared with that of other periods. The ready-made dress trade produces vast quantities of garments in standard sizes, and the untrimmed dresses of today take a comparatively short time to make.

New materials like nylon and perlon are far more durable than anything previously known and they are easily washed, so that fewer garments are needed. They are made of thread produced chemically, in contrast to the organic thread of wool, silk and cotton.

Clothes are, however, less important than they were, and women now spend much more money than they used to do on bodily exercise, on the care of the hair and on cosmetics, which came into general use in 1918.

Functionalist fashions gave women all the mobility advocated by the reformers of the last century. Both the costume and the contemporary products in furniture and housing, stripped of all embellishments, were believed to have achieved a kind of perfection. But style is a living thing, growing and maturing out of the past. It reaches full bloom often after facing fierce opposition, only to wither and die. What then has been the fate of Functional-ism, that puritanical, classically bare and somewhat severe style?

As mentioned above, in 1948–49 the New Look of Christian Dior sought to cover up the female legs by lowering the hem, which was not to be raised again to knee level for another ten years. In the late 1940s and early 1950s the focus shifted to the female bust—and not for the first time in modern history. One need only recall the dresses of the Rococo period with their deep décolletage. But in the 1950s the bust was not so much on display as given an exaggerated emphasis. Well padded elasticated and carefully designed bras-sières were calling enthusiastic attention to the undoubted fact that a woman is the possessor of a pair of breasts. The 'sweater girl' became the rage, her ideal measurements being: bust 38″, waist 24″, hips 34″. The emphasis on the bust was greatest in 1956 and went out of fashion soon after.

In the spring of 1957 Yves Saint Laurent, Dior's heir-apparent, presented his 'sack dress' (676), and his new trapeze line (678), the successor to Dior's 'H' line of 1955. In hiding and minimizing both waist and bust, the new styles foreshadowed radical innovations and flowing lines in the female dress (681). It was left to England, however, to give these new impulses their due as once before, during the French Revolution, she had pioneered in the development of fashion, both women's and men's.

From England we got the ever-skimpier dress and the high boots (679). From England, too, we got the 'little girl dress' (683). So great was its impact that the very concept of the grown or mature woman completely disappeared for a time. In the world of fashion the ideal woman—and every well-defined era chooses its own—became Twiggy, the British cover girl with her un-developed body, childishly straight hair, and girl-ish dress.

Although la garçonne, the boy–girl of Functional-ism, created in the years after the First World War, had also been young, indeed very young, at least she was a young woman. In search of a life away from the family, she stepped shyly into the world with a boyish figure and haircut, dressed in a knee-length outfit. But Twiggy was still younger, la garçonne's baby sister. Yet Twiggy, too, and her imitators departed from the norms of the parental world. Since the early 'sixties a rebellious mood

had turned an affluent youth against the cultural heritage of an older generation. Provos, hippies, flower children, flower power were some of the terms associated with young people in their attempt to create a new life style.

The youth rebellion and generation gap brought about a decisive break with the traditional male costume, which had remained largely unchanged since the turn of the century. From England The Beatles, on whom numerous others modelled themselves, went out to conquer the world of the 'sixties. Their beat music, with its Indian and African strains, took over from jazz and they also caused a revolution in dress and hair styles. Their long hair was an innovation (684) and if anything recalled the long hair of the mid-seventeenth century. Now that young people preferred to grow their hair shoulder-length, the cropped nape became a mark of dignity for the older generation, even though this hair style owed its origin to the military fashion of late eighteenth-century Prussia.

The new fashions for young people revived and developed the Art Nouveau style of 1890–1910. (Others may remember it best under its German name Jugendstil, 'the style of youth'). Art Nouveau enjoyed a brief and passionate career. Its possi-bilities apparently still unexploited, however, it was given a new lease of life. From 1968 we encounter the psychedelic patterns inspired by hallucinatory images and colours. Psychedelic decorations flourished in the patterns of materials (680, 688) and on the window-frames of tiny 'boutiques' throbbing to beat music—affluent youth's favourite haunts—which the teenage sections of department stores were desperately trying to imitate. Similar street decorations pro-voked some municipalities into prohibiting them as a species of urban unrest.

As the earlier Art Nouveau had been strongly influenced by the enthusiasm of the Impressionists for the art of Japan and her 'living line', so the new Art Nouveau was looking, even more emphatically, for exotic inspiration.

While the traditional Western male costume with its suit, collar, tie and polished shoes became the visible symbol of modernization and in-dustrialization to the developing nations, by con-trast Western youth, whose ideas would now seem to be determining the next stage in fashion, began to draw on a rich variety of foreign sources, often quite indiscriminately. They began tapping the colour schemes and dress styles not only of Japan but also of the American Indians, of India (*686*) and especially of her neighbouring countries, Afghanistan and Tibet.

Under British leadership the male hair grew longer and the traditional male dress began to show signs of dissolution. The female miniskirt grew steadily shorter while the dress with its matching, close-fitting, tailored same-length coat replaced the coat and skirt (*688*). Besides the miniskirt, women took to wearing trouser outfits consisting of either a sweater and jeans or a jacket and long trousers from the same material. At this point we were confronted with a new phenomenon, unknown since the early Gothic period when long tunics were worn by both sexes, namely, the look-alike trouser suit or unisex wear. With both sexes often affecting shoulder-length hair, only their voices would betray who was male and who was female.

The ultra-short female dress as well as the trouser suit, which as a one-piece suit might also serve for formal wear (*685*), greatly influenced the undergarment, always an important foundation for the visible dress. During the Renaissance and Rococo periods the corset and side-hoop served that purpose, as did the corset, drawers, and petticoat throughout the nineteenth century. When stockings were a constantly visible accessory and later the bust was emphasized, the brassière, panties and girdle became indispensable. Panty belts, worn under tights, followed just as predictably in the revealing wake of the miniskirt. The latest addition to the undergarment has been the elastic 'bodystocking', very similar to a bathing-suit. Together with the elastic panty belt it models the body gently without changing it or emphasizing any parts at the expense of others.

In the late 'sixties and early 'seventies a new development took place. The generous display of legs, regardless of their shapeliness, permitted by the miniskirt went out of fashion. Stockings with ever larger patterns and made of thick knitted fabrics in bright colours became the rage even if hidden under the trouser suit (*682*). Then in 1969–70 the first maxi-coats (*689*) made their appearance. The early models had a certain masculine military cut, reaching down to the ankle of the high boots, while helmet-like hats made the female head seem quite small at the top of the cylinder-shaped coat. More recently coats and dresses have tended to widen at the bottom, to shorten to 'midi-length' and to get tighter from the waist up. The lines of the coat have begun to give shape to the female figure at the same time that it dresses it in 'long skirts'. Its focus on the narrow waist is a portent for future fashion.

In conclusion, we may raise these questions: Will the female trouser suit—exhibited in such exciting variety in Asia whence part of today's fashion derives its inspiration—survive and undergo further development? Or will the *fin-de-siècle* tendency of the new *Art Nouveau* bring back the sexually differentiated costume where the male is dressed in a trouser suit and the female body is mysteriously hidden in long skirts? Or, as a third possibility, has the male trouser suit played itself out for the present and will the unisex tendency result in a new type of male tunic, recalling the earlier Gothic period with its tunic for both sexes? Or could it be that the new *Art Nouveau* will branch off in entirely novel directions? No definite answers are possible. A change in style, accompanied by shifting trends in fashion, never was and never will be predictable. Therein lies its vitality and its ability to surprise and persuade us.

INDEX

[The figures in italics refer to the numbers of the coloured plates, the figures in roman type to the pages of the text at the end of the book.]